iMPeRfect PARENTING

Connection OVER Perfection

By Brittney Serpell

TABLE OF CONTENTS

ENDORSEMENTS

I am so proud of my mom—she wrote a book! We have had some very hard times, and at one point I didn't think I could repair my relationship with my mom. But she continued to pursue me even when I didn't understand why. She is not just my mom but a role model I look to for how to choose connection in all my relationships. She gives 100 percent in everything she does and puts God and family as her priority. I am so proud to have her as my mom and thankful that our story can be a resource to help other families.

Delani Serpell
Daughter to Ben and Brittney Serpell
Age 17, currently in 12th grade

My mom has always put God and our family first. She is my biggest encourager and supporter of my dreams, but she also challenges me and gives me opportunities to grow. I hope that parents who read this book learn the importance of connection and communication. My mom has had such a big impact on my life and I know this book is filled with all the goodness she has brought to the family!

Adalyn Serpell
Daughter to Ben and Brittney Serpell
Age 13, currently in 7th grade

My mom is the best! She always helps me with stuff I struggle with, she is kind and always encouraging, and she has taught me how to be brave and courageous and how to forgive. One of my favorite things about her is that she has good boundaries and helps me protect my mind. I love that she is funny and helps our family have fun together. I hope that when you read this book you will learn to be kind and loving to your family. Ten out of 10 would recommend!

Lincoln Serpell
Son to Ben and Brittney Serpell
Age 10, currently in 5th grade

To my favorite people on the earth . . .

Ben, you make the best partner in the wildest journey we agreed
to take together.
Your love for God and family is like the roots to a great redwood—
it keeps us all connected to what is most important.

Delani, Adalyn, and Lincoln, you are rays of sunshine to our lives.
Our home would be void of so much joy without you.
You are each growing into inspiring humans.
It's an honor to be trusted by God to be your mommy.
I love you more than all the acorns that have ever fallen from
the oak trees on our farm.

ACKNOWLEDGMENTS

First, I want to thank my family. You have always been the greatest support, and this book would not be possible without you all. Ben, Delani, Adalyn, and Lincoln, I am so proud to be part of your world and I love you with the greatest, deepest love I have.

Mom and Dad, thank you for not settling with what you were given. You fought for something better, you searched for God's design for family, and you did all you knew how to give me and my brothers a fighting chance. We know nothing of the struggle you two came from because of your faithfulness to God and the sacrifices you made. I love you both—you are my heroes.

The LOP team! You are and will always be family! I don't think people truly understand the culture we have between us all. We may be a small group of people, but we are mighty. I have felt your strength in this whole process, from celebrating the first yes to the party that follows the completion of this book. I could not ask for a better group of people to have in my corner. I truly am honored to work alongside you.

Allison, girl, this whole thing would still be a dream if you had not been there with me. Getting lost in hours of conversation, working endless hours to meet deadlines—all in the best and wildest time of your life. Thank you for all that you gave to this project. You are a gift to me and so many! God has placed an anointing on your life to help others see what is trapped inside trying to become a resource. You help them, guiding them on the journey to seeing it become a real *book*! Irreplaceable. You are a wonderful person I love having in my life. I can't wait to do this again. We're gonna have so much fun!

There are so many others to mention. Jordan—you gave me a safe space to start. Thanks for being amazing! Banning, SeaJay, and the JC Family— what a beautiful church to have and a support in my life throughout the years. My friends—you know who you are. Thank you for staying close in the hardest season of my life. Thank you, thank you for believing in me!

FOREWORD

By Danny Silk

In my day, the primary challenges of parenting were sorting out the wrong friends, monitoring music selections, checking for drugs, and managing the new dynamics of how the internet chat rooms and MySpace were affecting our children. We had no idea what laid ahead of us or future generations.

Parents today are experiencing a world my generation knew nothing about. Cell phones, internet, video calls, social media, and whatever is coming with the "meta world" have created a type of distorted reality, access to information, and rate of change that stagger the grandparents of today. Add to this gender confusion, LGBTQ, unprecedented access to pornography, education systems spouting an anti-Christ foundation, every major media and entertainment source doing the same, and we have WWIII in the spirit realm in living color every waking day. The swirl of all these effects is driving anxiety through the roof in most families.

However, while the world has changed, people and relationship dynamics are strangely similar. Intense family dynamics are nothing new. Generational culture shifts and technology gaps aren't uncommon either. What is new is the level of disintegration in our family bonds. The connections between parents and children are in the crosshairs of our enemy and he seems much more effective today. The numbers of disconnected and divided families are mounting like cords of wood right before our eyes. Hopelessness of reconciliation between parents and children seems commonplace. Fatherlessness, abortion, divorce, sex trafficking, and domestic violence seem easy to identify and blame, but is anyone actually going to address the problem?

That begs the question: What is the problem? I've been known to be a master of oversimplification, but in this case I'll have to agree with Jesus. He gave us the solution to the problem that is tearing us apart today: love. We need systems and practices that make our homes, families, and marriages immune to the onslaught of social and economic woes. We must fear-proof our families with intense connections rooted in mature love. We know that a healthy host will not pick up the threats that are invading the unhealthy. We know that a dry field is susceptible to going up in flames with just the smallest spark and yet that same field saturated in moisture and plush with greenery isn't threatened by fire. Same field, same threat—what is the difference? The host environment is what makes the difference! Whole, healthy families are going to save the world!

Imperfect Parenting, this amazing book you are about to read by Brittney Serpell, will set you up to address the health and well-being of your home's environment. The way to build an immunity to the fearmongering world around us is to build a fear-proof family culture. Mature love prioritizes what matters most to our Father. Building a culture in our homes that mirrors the way our Father runs His home is what makes us a light in a dark world. For too long, Christian families have been famous for strict parental control and an overemphasis on punishment. In essence, we've become known for fear and limitations instead of our calling, which is to be known for how we love each other and the freedom we generate in those around us.

Imperfect Parenting is exactly that: no human being is perfect, nor will we ever raise one. Therefore, we must learn to overcome the fear of being out of control of these people who mean the world to us, and to separate their choices from our own identity. It's our fear that we reproduce into our own family culture. That fear, in turn, becomes a counselor to our children and sets them up to be easily manipulated by social pressure and trends. It's not our goal to control our children, but instead to teach them to control themselves and to believe that they can know and follow God confidently through the maze of choices in life. The skill of connection with God is first practiced in the home with us. We must be master teachers of connection in the home and yield young people into the world who know what mature love feels like, thinks like, and behaves like.

Sheri and I live with Ben and Brittney Serpell. We've watched them build a fearless family culture with children who know mature love. We watch these children love one another. We watch Ben and Brittney parent through the unexpected events of life and family. In numerous situations I've seen them do better than Sheri and I have done with our own children. Our respect for their accomplishments is the highest I know how to give. We live in a constant state of being impressed with this family. These stories you are about to read and learn from are real. I was there! The level of relational maturity and love they live in is impeccable.

As you read the following pages, I want to encourage you to receive an impartation for the value of connection. It is the primary element that makes it all work. When Jesus taught His disciples to pray, He said, "Your kingdom come and Your will be done on earth [in our homes] as it is in heaven [Your home]" (Matthew 6:10). Connection to our Father's heart and His priorities is paramount to bringing heaven to our families. Our success in building mature love in our homes will be the key to setting our children up to lead fearless lives and to build whole, healthy families for themselves to enjoy one day.

Peace to your house,
Danny Silk

1

The War of Connection

I'M GOING TO BE HONEST with you. For years, I felt nervous about writing a parenting book, for a couple of reasons.

For one, I'm still parenting three kids at home. Sure, we're long past the infant, toddler, and preschool years, so I'm not a total rookie, but the thing about parenting is that just when you think you're getting the hang of one stage of development, they move on to another one, and you feel like a novice again. Wouldn't it be better to wait till the kids have fully launched as adults to sit down and compile all my parenting advice? And really, with a high schooler, middle schooler, elementary schooler, husband, small family farm, and a full-time job, who has time to write a book?

For another, my dad, Danny Silk, already wrote a great book on parenting, *Loving Our Kids on Purpose*. I got pretty much all of my tools as a parent and family coach from him and my mom. What could I add to their teaching that would justify a whole new book on the subject? My life has enough pressure—there's no need for me to reinvent the wheel here.

And then we hit 2020 and 2021—two years that upended life as we knew it for almost everyone. As if marriage and parenting weren't hard enough for everyone, we had to throw a pandemic into the mix and add a few new extra challenges—working from home; setting up and monitoring home schooling; returning to school with masks and social distancing; coping with the cancellation of sports, performing arts, and many activities our kids were involved in; and the greatest challenge of all—trying to comfort, protect, and lead our kids in an anxiety-filled, divisive, confusing, and uncertain environment that we ourselves didn't understand, which was also testing the limits of our emotional, mental, and spiritual health.

I had multiple parents coming to me for family coaching appointments during those two years and confessing that they were losing it at home with their toddlers and young school-aged children like never before. "I thought I loved my four-year-old, but now that he can't go to daycare, I basically want to kill him." Other parents were at a loss trying to respond to teenagers whose mild acting out had suddenly escalated to asking to be put on antidepressants or hormones because they had decided they were now transgender. Marriages were strained to the breaking point; I can't remember any other two-year period in which I saw the connection between so many couples tested so intensely. Decisions over how to navigate holiday gatherings and other events caused significant damage to relationships with extended family members. Somehow this crisis got even Christians to contemplate walking away from lifelong friendships and relationships over their conflicting views . . . and some actually did just that.

THE ROOTS OF OUR DISCONNECTION

One of the strangest things about that crazy season was that, unlike other national crises or tragedies, like World War I and II, the assassinations of JFK and Martin Luther King, Jr., 9/11, or Hurricane Katrina, the COVID-19 pandemic didn't really bring people together. Historically in the face of a common threat, Americans have remembered that they're all part of a national family, set aside their differences, and rallied together to solve the problem. Instead, the atmosphere of fear and uncertainty hanging over everyone like a storm cloud only seemed to expose and exacerbate the *disconnection* that has been growing in our society for a long time. Many people labeled it as the cultural or political war between left and right, conservative and liberal progressive, Democrat and Republican, and many blamed a certain president for causing all these sides to suddenly become so hostile. But this connection problem goes far deeper, and has a much longer history, than whatever happened during those few years before and during the pandemic.

At the end of 2020, my dad and I decided to launch a new podcast together so we could speak to many of the things we were watching unfold from a biblical perspective and offer people courage, hope, and vision. In our planning conversations, we compared notes on what we were seeing take place in our family, relationships, church community, ministry networks, and the clients and audience we serve through Loving on Purpose. We both agreed that while the levels of fear, disrespect, control, and division we were seeing break out in people's lives were alarming and seemed to be affecting almost everyone we knew to some degree, this was not really a new or unprecedented attack on individuals, marriages, families, and society. This was just the latest skirmish in the war of connection we knew had been raging for decades.

Of course, according to the Bible, the war of connection began all the way back in the Garden of Eden. That's where humans first invited disconnection into their relationships with God, themselves, and each other through sin, and unleashed the fear that wars against love and connection into every human life. In many ways, the Bible is a history and spiritual diagnosis of how the war of connection has been raging in the human family since disconnection entered it—and the incredible steps God took over centuries to restore our connections with Him, ourselves, and each other.

3

In our own time and culture, the war over connection in our families took a turn for the worse during the Sexual Revolution of the 1960s, when contraception, free "love," and no-fault divorce all became widely available and were promoted, soon followed by legal abortion in 1973. All of these represented a major shift in the general understanding and definition of sex, dating, men and women, marriage, and the family. For the last fifty-plus years, we have been in a big cultural experiment to discover what happens when you attack the heart and integrity of the family, and by extension all our social connections, by telling people they can have sex without consequences, that they can come and go from marriages if they're happy or unhappy, and that "the kids will be all right" if we just turn them loose to experiment with sex, identity, and any behaviors or ideologies they like. And how is that working out for us? We now have generations of kids growing up in broken homes, a massive rise in teen pregnancies and high-risk behaviors associated with a lack of fathers, the abortion movement that has slaughtered sixty million babies in the womb, the toxic explosion of pornography and all other forms of sexual exploitation, a decline in marriage and birth rates, an educational, entertainment, and social media culture that robs children of their innocence and indoctrinates them in this new sexual culture from an early age . . . and the list goes on. Overall happiness levels have gone down as depression, anxiety, loneliness, and suicide have gone up. The general level of trust people feel for those around them has plummeted. So many people today—both Christians and non-Christians—are walking around with the deep desire to experience connection and belonging, and in their heart of hearts want to marry, have kids, and build a happy, healthy family. Yet accomplishing this desire feels daunting if not impossible due to the levels of insecurity, shame, and anxiety that almost everyone is carrying in some capacity due to how broken and disconnected we've become. Only if our goal is to destroy people's lives and society can we argue that this experiment is working.

REFUGEES TURNED WARRIORS

After fifty-plus years, every one of us has been affected by this chapter of the war on connection and the family. My grandparents participated in this new approach to marriage and had multiple marriages and divorces. As a result, my parents grew up in unstable homes with a single mom (my dad) and blended family (my mom), and came into marriage as relational refugees with trauma and a limited grid or tools for building a lasting, healthy marriage and family. What made the difference for them was that they both gave their lives to the Lord and joined a Christian community where they were able to watch people doing marriage and parenting according to the wisdom of the Bible. Their personal quest and battle to learn how to do marriage and family completely differently than what they grew up with not only created a brand-new experience for me and my two brothers, it ultimately equipped them with the wisdom and authority to help others struggling with the effects of family breakdown. They've been doing that work for decades now—traveling, speaking, writing books, working with church leaders, couples, and families all over the world on how to build loving, connected covenant relationships that will last for a lifetime and leave a legacy of love for generations to come.

Growing up in the Silk home meant that I got a front-row seat to watch my parents on the front lines of the war for connection in families, and would eventually be drafted and sent to the front lines myself. Before he became a pastor, my dad was a social worker, and for some years, we actually lived in a group home for foster youth. If you want to see one of the most tragic results of family breakdown in our society, spend some time with kids in the foster system. In high school, I accompanied my dad to many training events and watched him teach Love and Logic parenting tools (you'll be seeing plenty of these in this book) to desperate parents with homes full of disconnection and chaos. At sixteen, I became a nanny to two girls, six and seven, who were taken from their mother by Child Protective Services and sent to live with their father, who worked full time. It was my first experience working directly with kids from abusive home environments. After six months, their father came to me asking me to teach him what I was doing with his girls, because they actually listened to me!

At eighteen, I married Ben and we began our own journey of connection with each other and, two years later, with our first child, Delani. Adalyn joined us five years later, and Lincoln completed our family three years after that. In the next chapter, I'll get into some of the nitty gritty of our early years of marriage and how we learned to fight for and protect our connection—the struggle was real! Meanwhile, our work with families continued as we stepped into staff roles at Bethel Church—Ben in the youth department and me in the children's department. There we saw how pervasive disconnection and family breakdown were even in the church, and especially its effects on children, from toddlers to teens.

Soon after moving to Sacramento in 2013, Ben and I joined my parents on the Loving on Purpose team. For the last ten years, we've been putting in our reps working with young adults, couples, and families as teachers and marriage and family coaches (while still learning to apply all the principles we teach in our own marriage and parenting, of course). One of the things that both breaks our hearts and fuels our passion for the work we are doing is seeing how many young people are approaching the traditional adult milestones of dating, getting married, and raising children with wounds, baggage, and a broken framework for understanding how these relationships, roles, and responsibilities are even supposed to work. We have what has become an extremely rare story—we had no sexual partners before marriage and have been faithful in our marriage. For most young people in their teens and early twenties today, even in the church, that ship has already sailed before they've even had the opportunity to discover that there is another option than simply going along with whatever the wider culture is telling them to do. Thankfully, however, that's not the end of the story, and we are committed to helping as many people as we can untangle themselves from our culture of disconnection and begin to walk in the core values and practices of connection and God's design for our relationships and family.

THE WAR WITHIN

Two things finally tipped me to write this book—not including my dad, who had been nudging me to write it for years. The most important for me personally was that our family finally emerged from a very intense parenting season, which I will tell you about later in the book. While it was happening, it was definitely not the time for me to be focusing on teaching a wider audience, because I was in school myself learning to battle for connection in our family at a new level. But now we're through it and I have spoils of victory to share with you!

The second thing was watching how the war of connection unfolded during the years of the pandemic and how people were responding to it. Again, there has always been a war on connection—the pandemic just exposed it in a way that was unexpected and shocking for many. As marriage and family coaches, people usually call Ben and me when the war comes to their door in some undeniable way—they have a preschooler or elementary school kid who is literally terrorizing the house, an adolescent child who has discovered porn, a pregnant teenage daughter, or a revelation of infidelity, addiction, or betrayal that has devastated the marriage. During the pandemic, it seemed like the war showed up on pretty much everyone's door at the same time. It reminded me of this old Adam Sandler movie, *Click*, in which a dad gets a remote control that allows him to freeze and fast-forward through years of his life, forcing him to see all the issues that are building while he's not paying attention. Lockdowns essentially created a freeze-frame on many aspects of our lives that we had previously been ignoring and maneuvering around. We thought our marriages were in decent shape. We thought we knew how our kids were doing in school and what they were being taught. We thought we were doing an okay job preparing them for the future. We thought our spiritual and mental health were satisfactory. Suddenly, in the pressure cooker of fear, uncertainty, and big, uncomfortable changes, we discovered that none of these things were quite as healthy, strong, and intact as we thought.

When the war comes to our door, we have an opportunity and a choice to make. The opportunity is, will we recognize that the scary behavior coming out of the people around us or ourselves is not the real issue, but a symptom of the war of connection—the fruit of disconnection—in our closest relationships? And if we recognize this, will we choose to pursue healing for that disconnection? This is not an easy thing to do, because for most of us it means admitting that we've been more or less in survival mode and autopilot and not doing the things we need to do to fight for, build, and protect strong connections with God, ourselves, and others. It means changing the status quo and intentionally going after something better than what we've currently been operating from. That's going to take some work.

But if we don't take this opportunity or make this choice, I can tell you what will happen. We will actually continue to operate in disconnection and will ultimately add fuel to the fire that led to the issues confronting us. Let me explain.

The war of connection is a spiritual war between fear and love, and this war is fought in the heart of every human being. Fear drives us toward self-preservation, while love drives us toward connection. The goal of fear is survival, while the goal of love is thriving. So when we are operating out of fear, we instinctively adopt certain styles in our relationships, particularly in our parenting.

Many of us go into "perfect and control" mode, which says, "I'm scared of your messy behavior. Here come the lectures, rules, and punishments." Others of us go into "be your friend" mode, which says, "I'm scared of you rejecting me because you see me as the bad guy. Here come lots of freedom and attempts to get you to like me by giving in to your demands." And for some parents, the overwhelm and powerlessness they feel in the presence of their child's behavior and the chaos in their home simply takes them out, and they end up in a third style: "I give up."

Child psychologists actually have names for these three styles: authoritarian, permissive, and uninvolved parenting. If you look at them, they are basically versions of our "fight, flight, or freeze" instinctive reactions played out in our parenting. They are all driven by fear and self-preservation, and ultimately produce disconnection and fear in our children. I saw *a lot* of them showing up during the pandemic. Unless we stop and call an audible on ourselves, we are all going to be on a path of reproducing these behavior styles in our kids. Which means we'll end up raising a bunch of anxiety-driven perfectionists; entitled, narcissistic rebels; or depressed, checked-out slackers. Worse, if we don't start fighting for connection with our kids, we are surrendering them to be influenced and discipled by any other voices in the wider culture that make them feel heard, seen, and accepted.

There's a fourth style, however. Child psychologists call it authoritative parenting, which fits, but since it's kind of easy to confuse authoritative and authoritarian, in this book I am going to call it *engaged* parenting. Engaged parenting says, "I'm going to set the rules and enforce the consequences of your choices, but I'm going to pursue a heart-to-heart connection with you in the process." Engaged parenting is the style that communicates to our kids that we are not afraid of their mistakes, that they must learn from them, that they are powerful and responsible, and that they will have our love through the whole process of them growing up, even when it's messy and painful. The only way we can operate with this style is if we are driven by love and pursuing the goal of connection.

Now, I decided to call this book *Imperfect Parenting* because I think, especially for Christian parents, the thing that bumps us out of engaged parenting and into the other fear-driven styles is when we get triggered and go into "perfect and control" mode. Unless that's just me? Wives and mothers especially, I know, struggle with perfectionism. As Brené Brown explains, the message of shame, which she defines as *the fear of disconnection*, tells women, "Be perfect," while it tells men, "Never show weakness." Pretty much every mom I know or have coached has admitted to wrestling with the inner critic telling them they are not enough or not living up to the unspoken expectations of what it means to be a good parent. It's amazing what we will obsess over—I literally have to remind moms that just because their dishes aren't all clean and they didn't cook a delicious organic raw meal with no yellow-5 dye in it for dinner, and in fact their child had McDonald's chicken nuggets instead, they're not a bad mom. If we don't deal with that internal fear, we will end up in a perfectionist "fight" reaction that we project onto our kids. "If I can just scare you enough to make you stop having a meltdown in Target or talking back to me, then I won't have to feel that disappointment in myself." Or a perfectionist "flight" reaction that is simply avoiding, papering over, or dissociating from the fact that our child has now received three reports from school for bad behavior. Or a perfectionist "freeze" reaction where we just cave in, decide we're a failure, and check out on the couch binging Netflix while our kids finger-paint the walls. Whenever we react from fear, we lose the war of connection. If we want to win the war, we must lay down the goal of perfection and the tools of fear and control, and embrace the goal of connection and the tools of love.

To be clear, imperfect parenting doesn't mean we don't have standards of behavior we expect and even demand from our children. It doesn't mean we don't teach them truth and values—in fact, it means the opposite. Many parents today have, in the name of avoiding perfectionism and being too authoritarian, swung to the other extreme of permissiveness where they teach nonsense like "Do what feels right" and "Find your truth." This is not how we love our children and raise them in the way they should go. Rather, the goal in imperfect parenting, which is engaged parenting, is teaching our children to practice the high standard of behavior we require of them out of love, just as we are also seeking to learn how to live up to that standard out of love and not fear.

FROM SURVIVAL TO VISION

Living with a standard of love requires us to live with a vision. Again, the goal of fear is survival through self-preservation, while the goal of love is thriving through connection. The goal of survival doesn't inspire much vision for life. When you're in survival mode, you're barely able to see a day, or maybe even a few hours, in front of you, and your main thought is, *Don't die*. It's so easy to get into survival mode, especially at the beginning of your parenting journey, because having an infant is literally a survival exercise. You are sleep-deprived for days on end, and if you get a shower it's a miracle, because you are on constant watch keeping this baby alive. However, after that precious infant begins to sleep through the night, the goal changes, and it continues to change through every stage of that child's development. If you stay in survival mode and don't have a vision for how you are going to lead your child toward thriving in each of those stages, it's not going to happen. You're going to be living reactively instead of proactively, and the culture of your home will be set by whatever the loudest, most pressing need or want seems to be in the moment.

A classic parable about vision is the story of the three bricklayers. When asked what they were doing, the first said, "I'm laying bricks." The second said, "I'm building a wall." And the third said, "I'm building a great cathedral." Guess which bricklayer woke up most inspired to go to work every morning? If we want to truly give our all and our best to our kids, we need a great, inspiring vision that will carry us through from diapers to high school graduation and beyond. What is the cathedral you're building in your home? What does it look like for your child to not merely survive to adulthood but actually thrive in becoming a whole, healthy person who is deeply connected to God, him or herself, and your family members?

Another great story about vision is the biblical account of the twelve spies scouting out the Promised Land. Significantly, every one of those spies saw the same thing—a rich land filled with milk and honey, but also with giants. The ten spies, who were filled with fear, saw themselves as "grasshoppers" in the eyes of the giants, while Joshua and Caleb saw the giants as their "bread" because God was with them (Numbers 13:33; 14:9). The ten spread their fear through the entire Israelite camp, all but convinced them to go back to the land of slavery, and ended up causing an entire generation to wander and die in the wilderness. The two with vision, however, survived those forty years and led the next generation into the Promised Land. Caleb specifically asked for the territory of the giants to be given to him, and personally took them out one by one.

In the Promised Land of marriage and parenting, there is the milk and honey of love and connection to enjoy, but there are also giants of fear and disconnection to battle. What gave Caleb and Joshua the courage to pursue those giants? "The Lord is with us" (Numbers 14:9). This is what you need to know. If you are a parent, then God chose *you* for that child, and He is with you. When you anchor your heart and vision in connection with Him, you fight on the winning side in this war of connection. He is for you, your marriage, and your family.

If there's one thing I want to give you in this book, it's the vision to see your current assignment as a spouse and parent as something truly epic and worthwhile. Whether you are changing a diaper, helping your toddler get his shoes on the right feet, showing your elementary schooler how to clean his room, talking to your adolescent about sex, or taking your teenager to her first high school dance—if you are doing it from a heart of love with the goal of connection, you are not just laying bricks. You're building a cathedral. You're not just in an ordinary marriage raising ordinary kids who will go off and live ordinary lives. You're raising giant-killers. Ultimately, I believe, you are playing a crucial role in raising members of the next generation who will be part of turning the tide in the war of connection in our society.

We hear a lot these days about "being on the right side of history." What I can tell you with certainty is that fighting for our families to live in connection and in the goodness of God's design for our relationships is the right side of history. If the Bible diagnoses disconnection with God, ourselves, and others as the root of family breakdown, on the positive side it reveals our original design to live in connection, and the incredible, supernatural power of God's love we receive through Jesus, which restores our ability to live in connection. These aren't just theological concepts. It is an obvious, practical reality that God's design for the human family—a husband and wife who love well and raise their kids to love well and grow up and form loving families of their own—is what produces both whole, healthy individuals and a whole, healthy society. Everything we see breaking down in our society—from our mental-health crisis to the drug crisis to crime to the economy and everything else that's falling apart—is ultimately rooted in the breakdown of the family and connection. But the good news is that the relational devastation we've seen since the Sexual Revolution is not the end of the story. God is on the move, calling person after person, couple after couple, and family after family to reject the broken story of the world and step into His hope-filled story of family restoration. As He did with my parents, He is turning the relational refugees and walking wounded of the war of connection into warriors who will fight for themselves, their children, and their children's children to know and walk in this better story. He is building whole, healthy families out of the rubble, and Whole, Healthy Families Are Going to Save the World. (Yes, that's the tagline for our podcast, *The KYLO Show*.)

I want you to become one of those warriors. I want to call and inspire you to believe that no matter what has been broken or lost in your own journey of connection and family, you can be restored. In fact, the very thing the enemy has tried to steal from you is where the Lord wants to give you authority over him.

You *can* be a husband and wife who see each other as a partnership and a unity and are so madly in love that you have value for all of your differences and quirks.

You *can* look at your kids, see heaven's design in each one of them, and step into the privilege of helping them develop, mature, and grow so that they can go into the world walking closely with the Lord and doing what He created and called them to do.

You *can* be a connected, thriving family that enjoys each other and participates in a strong culture of love in your home and wherever you go.

And through all this, you *can* be part of "[rebuilding] the ancient ruins and [raising] up the age-old foundations" (Isaiah 58:12 NIV) of our culture and society. This is what you were made for.

Don't worry, this book is not going to major on sociology, theology, or even parenting techniques, though there's some of each of those in the pages ahead. But mainly I'm going to tell you our story—specifically, the story of how Ben and I went from being "babies having babies" to learning how to win the war of connection in our home by intentionally cultivating the family culture we want, based on the wisdom we have received from others and the vision we have pursued from the Lord. As I said, we still have kids at home, so this culture-building project is an ongoing process. But as I finally realized when I said yes to writing this book, that's what the work of family always is—if it's working. There's no arriving. There's only moving on to the next lesson and giving away whatever you learned in the last one.

2

The Story of Us

BEFORE I START SHARING THE Saga of the Serpells, I want to remind you that our story is just one family story among hundreds of thousands of family stories. What unites every family story on earth is not the particular configuration of father, mother, children, and extended family members, but the fact that we are all on a journey of connection, of growing up and learning to be human beings within a network of important relationships. While some are blessed to grow up in families that are healthier and more intact, no family or individual gets to escape the effects of the war of connection. Since the fall, no marriage, parent, or family has perfectly reflected the divine family of Father, Son, and Holy Spirit in whose image we were created. Adam and Eve were rebellious, one of their sons killed his brother, and the mess and drama just continued from there. So as you're reading our story, resist the urge to compare it to your story in externals. I'm hoping you'll find plenty to relate to in the story, but don't trip over whatever you can't relate to. Whether you're single, married, divorced, or remarried; whether you're parenting with the mother or father of your children or you're co-parenting or step-parenting; or whether you're in a traditional nuclear family, a broken family, or a blended family, you have the same basic challenge as we do in our family and as anyone else has—to learn how to pursue a healthy, loving connection and overcome the fear and the urge to self-protect, control, and perfect that war against this goal.

MY FIRST BATTLE WITH PERFECTIONISM

So let me take you back to a time long, long ago in a place far away . . . to the days of Brittney the sixteen-year-old. That was the year my parents decided to move from the small town of Weaverville, California, where I'd lived most of my life, to be the Family Life pastors at Bethel Church in Redding, California.

It was a huge deal for me to move in the middle of high school and leave all my friends from school and church behind. On top of that, my parents told us kids we had to keep the move a secret until they could announce it publicly. Knowing that this transition was coming and not being able to talk about it with the important people in my life outside my family was extremely tough on my heart. Then I had to say goodbye to everyone and start over in a new city, school, and church as a pastor's daughter who, like most pastors' kids, had gotten the message that it wasn't okay for me to struggle or have any problems. I was supposed to be Brittney Silk, the model child to whom every parent and family was looking as an example.

The whole situation was a massive setup for me to get disconnected from my own heart, from God, and from my family—and that's exactly what happened. I began to suffer the pain of loneliness like I never had before, and so I began trying to fill that void like so many people do . . . by talking to strangers on the internet. After a couple months of chatting with a seventeen-year-old boy from Sacramento, we made plans to meet up for a secret date in Redding one Saturday. I was completely naive about the dangers of doing something like this, but thankfully the guy turned out to be who he said he was. We hung out for the day, went out to eat, saw a scary movie (which I hated), and then drove to a park to make out by my car.

Out of nowhere, I heard a voice saying my name through the window of a car that had just pulled into the otherwise empty parking lot where we were. "Brittney!" I ignored it, but the person said it again. Breaking away from my date, I looked up and saw the face of our long-time family friend Kris Vallotton staring down at me.

Oh boy . . .

Long story short, that put an end to my date. I soon found myself sitting beside Kris's wife, Kathy, as she drove me home in my car—I was trembling too badly to drive—while Kris followed us. On the way, I called home and my father answered.

"Hey, Dad, it's me."

After a pause, I heard him say in a shaky voice, "I was just on the other line telling the police what you looked like."

"I'm fine," I said. "I'm safe. I'm with Kris and Kathy. I'll be home in a minute."

When I walked through the door, my dad directed me to wait on the couch while he and my mom talked with the Vallottons (I later learned that God had told Kris exactly where I was and how to find me) and sent my brothers to bed. When they finally came in to the living room, my mother worked hard to rein in her anger over what I'd put her through—she'd had a terrifying day trying to track me down and imagining the worst—while my dad refrained from lectures and instead asked me, "What's going on? What are you doing?"

Soon, all the pain and disconnection that had been growing inside me from before the move came spilling out. "You have no idea the pressure I feel to be your kid," I told them. "I have to be perfect. I can't make any mistakes ever, for my whole life. And then we come here and I have no friends. I don't know what to do. And I'm so lonely. I don't even want to be a Christian anymore."

The silence that fell after this statement sucked all the air from the room. At last, my father got down, crawled toward me, put his hands on my knees, and began to weep. "If what I do for a living is too much for you, I will quit tomorrow and go back to being a social worker. I can get a job anywhere. My only goal in life is that you and your brothers are with your mom and me on the other side."

This was the *last* thing I expected. What sixteen-year-old is told by her father that she has the power to tell him to abandon his career for her sake?

"I don't want you to quit your job," I sighed. "I just . . . I don't want to do this. And I'm tired. Can I go to bed now?"

And so we went to bed. The next morning was Sunday and everyone went to church except me. I was sitting on the couch watching *Ten Things I Hate About You* when my dad walked through the door.

"Coming to check on me?" I asked as my dad sat down beside me.

"No," he said. "I just didn't want to be far away from your heart." With that, he settled in beside me and we watched the movie together.

Now, my parents did take away my car, phone, and computer for a while as a consequence of me violating their trust. But they continued to pursue connection with me, and they also allowed me to keep dating this boy, who drove up to Redding every Saturday for several months to see me. Our dates took place primarily in the living room, and our goodbyes in the evening were observed by my father, who lingered conspicuously by the garage door after taking our dog Libby out to her kennel for the night. But both my parents understood that forbidding me absolutely from seeing him would not be good for our connection. So they let me explore this relationship with a guy, who was not a Christian, and prayed their best prayers that I would come around.

A few months after that fateful secret date, my mom and I made a trip to Sacramento to have dinner with my new boyfriend and his parents and then pick up my friend Ben from Australia. Ben had first come to the US to visit our youth pastor in Weaverville two and a half years earlier, when I was fourteen. We completely hit it off during the six weeks he was in town and even felt a bit of a romantic spark, but though we had stayed in touch ever since, nothing more had developed beyond friendship, and I didn't expect that to change. Ben was my "bro," I assured my boyfriend, and accordingly showed up to meet him at the airport in a T-shirt with messy hair and no makeup, feeling no need to impress. Imagine my surprise when a taller, much more manly seventeen-year-old Ben came down the escalator to meet me. While he was getting his bag, I surreptitiously borrowed my mom's purse and ran to the bathroom to put on some of her makeup to make myself more presentable. As we made the two-and-a-half-hour drive back to Redding, I couldn't stop giggling over this new grownup Ben . . . and how much I liked him.

By the next Sunday, things came to a head. The previous weekend, I had brought my new boyfriend to church for the first time, and while he seemed to be open-minded about it all, he clearly had no idea what was going on. Ben entered worship like a fish in water. The contrast between these two young men arrested me and confronted me with the truth. Ben was the kind of man I had always wanted, because he loved Jesus like I—the real Brittney—loved Jesus. The person I had been pretending to be with my new boyfriend was a fraud. Suddenly overwhelmed, I left the service and ran to the prayer chapel on Bethel's campus, where I completely fell apart. Sobbing, I poured my heart out to God, repenting for walking away from Him and my true self, and begging Him to let me marry Ben, because I just knew that Ben was what I needed to be able to be a Christian and serve Him like I wanted. When my tears were spent, I returned to the sanctuary and stood at the back, where my father met me. I hugged him sincerely for the first time in four months and we both cried because we knew—I was back.

Thankfully Ben felt the same way about me—apparently he had been telling people back in Australia that he was going to marry me. So I ended things with my internet boyfriend and Ben and I became official.

Thankfully we didn't have to do the long-distance thing for too long either. Six months after we got together, Ben's whole family decided to move to Redding so he and his parents could go to the school of ministry at Bethel. A year later, we both graduated—me from high school and him from his first year of ministry school—and the day before my eighteenth birthday in June, Ben proposed. We planned a wedding in three and a half months, and on October 18, 2003, Ben and Brittney Serpell launched out into the world to love each other, make babies, serve God, and do great things.

UNEXPECTED EXPECTATIONS

In *Loving Our Kids on Purpose*, my dad tells his side of this whole story and wraps it up with "Ben came from Australia, rode in on his white pony, swooped [Brittney] up, and they are living happily ever after."[1] To be fair, by the time that book came out, Ben and I were six years or so into our marriage and had just started to figure out how to really fight for and protect our connection, so "happily ever after" isn't too much of an exaggeration. But getting there was not a walk in the park.

As it turned out, my struggle with the expectation to be perfect did not magically go away after my parents showed me they didn't expect that from me and their goal was connection. That experience certainly set a standard in my life, a touchpoint that anchored me to the truth that the true war in life was the war of connection, and that was how battles were won. But we are all imperfect people living in an imperfect world, so the opportunities to trip over an expectation for things to be perfect are endless. In fact, I had all kinds of expectations of myself and of Ben that I didn't even know I had until those expectations weren't being met. And as these unmet expectations began to crop up, I began to be confronted with my own default

---

[1] Danny Silk, *Loving Our Kids on Purpose* (Shippensburg, PA: Destiny Image Publishers, 2008), Kindle Edition, 175.

toward perfectionism and how it derailed me from pursuing the goal of connection.

In every marriage you have realities that create stress and pressure—the responsibilities of building and managing a household, jobs, and kids together; the dynamics created by two very different personalities interacting; and the fact that both people involved are human beings on a learning journey that involves plenty of mistakes and failures. All of these stressors create endless opportunities for our fear and insecurities to be triggered and our go-to fight/flight/freeze reactions to come to the surface. And when you get married really young, like Ben and I did, it means that you are completely clueless about all of this. So at some point you have to realize what's going on and choose to grow up together, or allow your fear and immaturity to rip you apart.

When it came to managing responsibilities, neither Ben nor I had lived on our own or supported ourselves prior to marriage, so we had a lot of basic "adulting" to learn. Jobs, rent, banking, budgeting, laundry, cleaning—all of it. Like many young couples starting out, money was tight for us in those early years. Ben couldn't even work for the first six months of our marriage because he was still waiting for his green card, and then we were both only eligible for entry-level jobs.

One of the most difficult things for me personally that first year was that I went on birth control and gained fifty pounds before I finally realized I should get off of it. Then, one month after our first-year anniversary, I discovered I was pregnant with Delani. Two years into marriage, I was twenty years old, struggling to care for a newborn, seventy pounds heavier than my wedding day, and feeling completely ashamed of my body and unattractive to my husband. Nothing I did seemed to help me lose the weight, either. By the time Delani was a year old, I was still wearing my stretchy pregnancy jeans.

Along with my growing fear that I was failing as a wife because of my body, I also found that parenting my own child was much different from anything I had experienced working with other kids. I really thought that after growing up with the Love and Logic tools from the time I was eight years old or so, using them constantly on my brothers, the kids I babysat, and even my peers at school, I knew how to handle myself in the presence of a child. But as I soon realized with Delani, none of those previous scenarios had involved serious sleep deprivation and total, 24/7 responsibility for the child I was dealing with. Suddenly Miss "I've been to a million parenting seminars with my dad, worked with kids for ten years, and am widely regarded as a super-nanny" realized, *I don't know what I'm doing.* This child pushed buttons in me I didn't even know I had, and I found myself reacting to her in anger in ways I had never imagined I would. It was very disconcerting.

I also was surprised to feel some shame and insecurity when I discovered that, while I loved Delani to death and absolutely enjoyed being her mom, I wasn't totally satisfied or at my best simply by being a full-time parent. Nearly all of my closest friends during that season of life were stay-at-home moms who only ever wanted to be stay-at-home moms. They seemed perfectly content just momming day in and day out. That was not me. I liked balancing parenting with other part-time work, and I found that I was a happier and better mom for doing so. Parenting, especially parenting children under school age, requires you to be comfortable with mess, able to create routines but also be flexible, and fully alert and engaged with your child most of the time. This is a demand that we must all meet, regardless of our personality types, and thankfully those preschool years don't last forever (even though it can feel that way). However, certain personality types are more comfortable with the demands of parenting young children than others, something I didn't yet understand but instinctively sensed as I compared myself with my stay-at-home mom friends. In my case, being able to do some work out of the home where the expectations were clear, success was achievable, and I was able to interact with other adults helped me feel better and refueled my energy to get back in the trenches with my toddler.

Technically, I had to work to support us until Ben was able to work full time, but even after I had Delani, I continued to work part time as a nanny, receptionist, barista, and in other roles until I eventually came on staff at Bethel in the children's department. However, for many years I worked with a lingering fear that I *should* have been content just to stay home full time with Delani.

Over time, I began reacting to all this accumulating body and mommy shame by pulling away from intimacy with Ben, because I assumed he must judge my body as harshly as I judged it, and by pouring myself into trying to become the perfect mom for my daughter, because I felt like that was maybe something I could figure out and be good at. Worst of all, I took my fear, insecurity, and frustration with myself out on my husband.

This was surprisingly easy to do, because like most spouses do soon after getting married, I discovered that Ben and I had very different, indeed opposite, personalities. I just didn't understand why Ben couldn't seem to do things like me, whether it came to folding towels (we had a weird linen closet and the towels only fit when you folded them a *certain* way), to cleaning out the garage so my car would fit, to the way he was feeding Delani her rice cereal and bananas in the morning. Obviously my way was right and his was wrong, and I let him know this. The criticism I doled out to him seemed like nothing compared to the criticism that was constantly running in my own head toward myself, so it barely registered that I was attacking my words-of-affirmation-love-language husband right at his core.

But what really fueled my sense of justification in attacking Ben was finding out that my white-knight husband who had rescued me from the wayward path I had started down at sixteen was also not what I expected. He was, in fact, a human being who made mistakes. The one that really got the fear train rolling for me was when Delani was about six months old and we received news that the government was planning to deport Ben because he had forgotten to reapply for his INS papers. He had just started a job but had to stop working completely until the situation was rectified, which took about three months. I was shocked and shaken that my husband could overlook something so important, which hurt us financially and had the potential to leave me as a single mom for who knows how long until he could immigrate back to America. This was when mistrust first began to grow in my heart toward him and his ability to take care of me and our family. After that, I pretty much took over anything involving paperwork, and Ben became my secretary and to-do-list person.

Another time, when Delani was around two years old, I woke abruptly to the sound of the school bus honking loudly outside our door. Realizing I had overslept and Ben had already left for work, I flung myself out of bed in a complete daze and began scouring the house for Delani. Panicking when I realized she was not in the house, I threw on a sweater and headed for the front door. There waiting to meet me was my daughter, clad in a sagging diaper and accompanied by my neighbor, who explained that Delani had apparently opened the front door and the gate to the yard and had been out on the sidewalk greeting the bus as it arrived to pick up the neighborhood kids for school. The storm of fear and shame that erupted inside me was fierce. Of course I didn't want to face the fact that I had overslept and bore some responsibility for this walkabout toddler. Ben hadn't locked the front door—it was clearly his fault.

And then the day came when my good, honest husband confessed to me that he had been struggling with using porn for some time. Of course, this did nothing to help with my body shame or with the cycle of withholding myself, taking my self-criticism out on Ben, or grabbing control and responsibility away from him because he obviously couldn't be trusted to handle them in our relationship. It only poured more fuel on the fire, which in turn made Ben feel even more ashamed himself, more apprehensive about ever being vulnerable with me, and more frustrated that he couldn't figure out how to meet my needs.

THE TURNING POINT

About five years into marriage, Ben and I both recognized that if we didn't find a better way to get and stay connected, we were probably not going to make it for the long haul. We both wanted to build a great marriage, but the way we were interacting was basically keeping us in survival mode. Every good deposit we put in our relational bank account was soon burned up by stressful arguments. So we scheduled a meeting with my dad to talk about how frustrated we were with each other. Ironically, the very morning of our appointment, I learned that I was pregnant with Adalyn, which Ben and I still laugh about, because given the state of our sex life at that point, it was a mystery how that even happened.

My dad, as he always does, asked us some really great questions and helped us start to get a handle on what was driving the dysfunctional cycle in our marriage. It basically came down to the fact that we both needed to grow in emotional awareness and intelligence so we could recognize our go-to fear reactions—mine was aggressive (fight) and Ben's was passive (flight)—stop and reflect instead of running with them, and figure out how to communicate and meet our real needs in a place of trust and safety.

For my part, I needed to stop blaming Ben for everything that I felt was wrong in our life. Showing up as a controlling perfectionist he could never please was only going to continue to disempower him and discourage him from even trying to move toward me, which meant I was completely sabotaging what I actually wanted in our marriage. I didn't want a husband who was walking on eggshells, opting for passivity because it was safer than risking making a mistake and triggering my frustration. I wanted a partner who was going to offer strength I could lean on, but clearly I didn't know how to ask for one or make room for Ben to function that way in our relationship. To do that, I needed to figure out how to become a safe place for him to bring his strength, to have needs, to carry responsibility, and to make mistakes without the fear of punishment.

Ben, for his part, needed to start confronting me when I crossed the line of disrespect with my criticism and anger, and start showing up with his need to feel powerful, respected, and trusted.

I will never forget the day when my husband finally stood up to me directly. It was just after Adalyn was born, and we were driving across town to visit my parents. We were running late, and I decided to offer up some classic Brittney criticism about how Ben was at fault for this situation.

The next thing I heard was, "I would love to have this conversation with you as soon as your voice sounds like mine."

I looked over at Ben in shock. He wasn't looking at me. He just kept driving, pretending I wasn't there. "What did you say?" I asked indignantly.

"I would love to have this conversation with you as soon as your voice sounds like mine," he repeated.

Thanks to my upbringing in the Silk household, I knew exactly what Ben was doing. He was reading from the script that clearly told me, "You're being so disrespectful that I don't even want to talk to you right now." I couldn't believe it. I was so stunned and furious that he had called me out that I was tempted to do something completely irrational. I remember thinking, *I'm going to open the door to this car and just throw myself out.* Ben later told me, "I thought for sure you were going to hurt me." Instead, I just sat there fuming in silence until we reached my parents' house.

Once I began to simmer down and reflect on what Ben had just done, I realized that (1) my husband was now the first person after my own parents who had ever confronted my disrespect *in the moment* and required me to be respectful, and (2) I *had* been disrespectful. Typically, Ben would stoically (passively) endure me going off on him about something and then wait for me to come back and apologize for it, which I always did with some "but" to excuse and justify my behavior. This had obviously never led to me actually changing and finding a respectful way to communicate my frustrations and needs. Now Ben had drawn a line in the sand, and once I recognized the courage in his choice to require respect from me, it inspired me to respect him. It was a turning point in our relationship. Things didn't all instantly change—they never do—but it was a breakthrough we could start building on. From that point we made steady progress in dismantling the tracks of aggression and passivity we had laid down in our marriage, and started to lay new tracks of approaching one another consistently with the goal of connection.

Ben's growth in showing up as a powerful, responsible man, leader, husband, and father—and my growth in trusting him to do that—was such a gift to me and our family. As I realized I could stop expecting myself to carry the weight of both my responsibility and his, and that I could in fact lean on his strength and support, my stress and fear of failure began to lessen, and I began to be much more relaxed. This was especially evident in our parenting. Before he started standing up to me, Ben had also defaulted to passivity in his relationship with Delani. This created a pattern where, when I was with her, I would set boundaries and confront disrespect, but when Ben had her, he'd relax the rules and she'd come back to me thinking she could get away with anything. It was a recipe for me to continue to feel frustrated with both my daughter and my husband, especially since their behavior made me feel like I was failing as a wife and mom. But after Ben started to get courageous with me, he did the same with our daughter, and the two of us finally started to become a united front as parents. Being able to show consistency in our expectations, boundaries, and the behavior we were modeling for our kids eliminated so many of the behavior swings we had been wrestling with.

As Ben and I started to get healthier and more connected, I also began to work on my physical health. During Adalyn's pregnancy, I was diagnosed with gestational diabetes. I immediately fell down the tunnel of shame, feeling that I had failed by making choices that were causing my body to break down and quit on me right when I needed it to support the life of a child.

But it was also the wakeup call I needed. For the sake of my unborn daughter, my family, and myself, I knew I needed to make some changes and do all I could to move toward better health. For the whole pregnancy, I carefully watched my diet, exercised as much as I could, and monitored my weight. When Ady was born, the doctors told me it was a miracle she was alive, let alone completely healthy as she was, as her placenta had separated into pieces in the womb. I could only imagine how much worse it could have been if I hadn't done all I could to take care of myself during the pregnancy.

Because I succeeded in gaining only eighteen pounds with Ady, I actually left the hospital already back at my pre-pregnancy weight. Seeing the results of my discipline motivated me to continue losing weight and getting fit, though it wasn't until after I had Lincoln that I finally succeeded in getting almost all the weight off I had gained since my wedding. And because I had not only been working on my physical health over those years but also on my emotional and relational health with Ben, by the time Lincoln joined our family, we had become two much healthier, more self-aware, and consistently connected parents.

Taking care of my body was a ton of hard work, but it felt so good to break out of the powerless shame cycle of feeling uncomfortable, self-conscious, unattractive, and hopeless to change. Feeling more comfortable and confident in my own skin was great for my marriage, and feeling healthy and energized meant I could handle keeping up with my kids and my position in the children's department. In every area of my life, I could see the benefits from my choice to pursue my physical health.

There was one unexpected test that came out of that pursuit, however. I was sitting in church one day when I received a text from my personal fitness trainer. My eyes widened as I took in the very personal, very flattering, and very inappropriate message on my phone screen. In that moment, it dawned on me, *This is probably the moment where some people make the choice to have an affair.* My next thought was that, thanks to all the work we had put into our marriage over the four years or so since that day we met with my dad,

Ben and I were so deeply connected that I couldn't even comprehend making that choice. Instead, I showed him the phone and said, "I don't want to do anything with this but I want you to do something with it."

Ben scheduled a meeting with my trainer, who was half a foot taller, ten years older, twice as big, and covered with chiseled muscles. In the kind but direct manner that had now become normal for him, Ben said, "I need to know if you are going to protect my wife from you, because if you can't, we're done." My trainer was instantly apologetic and reassured Ben that he would be nothing but professional and respectful with me. Unfortunately, but unsurprisingly, I found that it just wasn't the same working with him after that, and I soon moved on to someone else. But I will always be thankful to him, in a way, for the opportunity he created for Ben and me to choose to protect us, and especially to affirm that I now had the strong partner I had begged God for all those years before in the prayer chapel.

REDEFINING PERFECTION

In the next chapter, I'm going to go deeper into some of the specific tools Ben and I used to build our emotional self-awareness and shift out of fear-driven reactions and into courageous, love-driven responses in our interactions. Above all else, it was walking through this process of becoming self-aware and learning how to meet one another's needs that caused us to mature out of survival mode and move toward being able to lead ourselves, our marriage, and our kids with purpose and vision. In the last decade-plus of coaching married couples, I have seen that the issue of self-awareness and meeting needs is the central problem affecting most marriages. This is the front line in the war of connection in your home, and it is what you and your spouse do about that front line that largely determines the experience you create for your kids. Whenever a parent or couple comes to me with a parenting issue, inevitably we trace it back to something that's broken or not working well in the marriage connection, or a problem in our level of self-awareness (often, these are connected).

But in order to truly confront our lack of self-awareness, we must also confront the system of beliefs that drives us toward the goal of perfectionism and away from the goal of connection. At its core, perfectionism is a need to cover our imperfections—to paper over, ignore, avoid, and dissociate from them rather than look at them with honesty, compassion, acceptance, and desire for improvement. It is the compulsion to control how things look on the outside instead of dealing with the messiness going on in our hearts. It's the demand that our expectations are the only ones that matter, which is really the demand that we be God in our own lives. It's ultimately rooted in shame and the fear of punishment, so its goal is always self-preservation, not vulnerability and connection. It's the enemy of self-awareness and sacrificial self-giving, which are the essential elements of mature love.

If you struggle with perfectionism like me, then one of the most critical things you must do if you want to win the war of connection in your life, marriage, and family is to allow God to redefine perfection and every expectation you have in your life for yourself, your spouse, and your kids. And the first expectation most of us need to start with is this: *God doesn't expect us to be perfect.* Or to be more precise, He doesn't expect us to be perfect the way we think of "perfect." Jesus did say "be perfect" (Matthew 5:48), but He meant something completely different from what most of us think it means to be perfect.

When I was sixteen, I thought I wasn't allowed to make mistakes. I thought that's what God and everyone else expected of the pastor's kid, and of Christians in general. That's what I thought it meant to be perfect, and that's what I think most of us think too. We may say we know God forgives us and doesn't expect us to be perfect, but deep down we're super afraid of making mistakes. So when I lost my temper with Delani or was mean to my husband or fell short in any way, I was immediately hit with shame for not living up to that expectation and standard. It wasn't until I truly started to surrender my expectations and replace them with God's actual expectations for my life that I started to break out of the cycle of making mistakes, feeling shame, beating myself up, and striving even harder out of shame to stop making mistakes.

Perfection has never been something we can preserve or achieve by not making mistakes. True, biblical perfection is a *process* that God is directing in our lives, and learning from our mistakes and messes is very much a part of that process. Biblical perfection means "mature, complete, lacking in nothing." Perfection lies on the other side of a long journey of growing up to be who we were created to be. What God expects from us is simply that we will take that journey with Him. We don't have to try to be perfect, because *He is perfecting us through our connection with Him.* As a loving Father, He is committed to walking with us, teaching us, and giving us all we need to become like Him, but the foundation for that whole process is our connection with Him. This is why His primary goal with us and expectation for us is connection.

When we accept that God's goal and expectation is a connection with us that produces transformation, it begins to shift our understanding of what He expects for all of our relationships. He doesn't expect us to have it all together when we get married or have children. Everyone is always complaining that husbands, wives, and babies don't come with training manuals. That's the point. We're all rookies on a journey to mastery, but what we are learning to master are not all the externals of "adulting." We are in a school of connection while in a war of connection. The sooner we lock on to this as our expectation and our goal, the sooner we will start to understand the journey we're on as spouses, parents, and family, how to make progress on that journey, and how to measure success.

3

God's Design for Family

IN *MERE CHRISTIANITY*, C. S. LEWIS helps to distill this truth that God does not expect us to be perfect and never make mistakes, but He does expect us to let Him perfect us—that is, to make us whole, mature, and complete in Him—as we walk in a connected relationship with Him. He says:

> . . . this Helper who will, in the long run, be satisfied with nothing less than absolute perfection, will also be delighted with the first feeble, stumbling effort you make tomorrow to do the simplest duty. As a great Christian writer (George MacDonald) pointed out, every father is pleased at the baby's first attempt to walk: no father would be satisfied with anything less than a firm, free, manly walk in a grown-up son. In the same way, he said, "God is easy to please, but hard to satisfy."[2]

This is how we need to think of God's expectations for us in our journey of connection, marriage, and parenting. As I reminded you at the beginning of the last chapter, there are no perfect people and no perfect families on the planet.

---

[2] C. S. Lewis, *Mere Christianity* (New York: HarperCollins, 2001), 202-203.

None of us gets to feel superior or inferior about where we're starting this journey. None of us is disqualified, and none of us gets to skip the journey because we're already qualified. God's definition of success for us is simply that we take the journey, and He is thrilled, like Lewis says, by every small step we take on it.

But that also means there is a way we can fail, and that is simply by not taking this journey of transformation and maturity, by refusing the call to learn how to fight in the war of connection. The parable of the talents is the classic biblical illustration of this. The master gave each of his servants resources and opportunities—each according to his ability—and all that mattered to him was that they used them. The bad servant failed because he refused to even try to engage in achieving his potential. He chose cowardice and self-preservation over getting in the arena and taking some risks to figure out how to make the most of his life. This is what we must not do. We are neither fated nor allowed to settle for where we are, because God has *more* for all of us, and He won't be satisfied until we are walking in the fullness of His design for us as individuals and family members.

When my parents said yes to their own journey of maturity as believers, as a husband and wife, and as parents, they had never really seen anyone in their family stay together in marriage for the long haul. They hadn't seen anyone in their family parent with tools of engagement and connection rather than fear and control. But when they joined the family of God; discovered God's design for connection, marriage, and family revealed in the Bible; saw people living in that design to a greater degree and thriving in it; and experienced the power of the Holy Spirit to help them start to live in that design themselves, their hunger for *more* was awakened, and they said yes to the journey. Was it easy? Not at all. But after thirty-plus years of putting in the blood, sweat, and tears of endless reps learning to move from fear to love, from disconnection to connection, and from self-preservation to covenant sacrifice, my parents have accomplished what no one in their family has. Now they—and their kids and grandkids—are living in a completely different experience than what they grew up with. They have proven to Ben and me that change is possible, which gives us tremendous hope, but also a sense of responsibility and accountability—both for our own marriage and family, and for those we are trying to coach, equip, and encourage. If they can do it, we all can. No excuses.

THE FAMILY IS THE IMAGE OF GOD

So what is God's design for connection, marriage, and family, and what does maturity in living in that design look like? If we're going to go on a journey of growth, we need to be able to measure that growth against a standard. None of us and none of our families have arrived at perfection, however, so we can't look to ourselves for that standard. We need to go to the source. So while I know I said this book wasn't going to major on theology, I need to take a few moments to refresh our memories on what the Bible tells us about God's design for connection, marriage, and family.

Scripture tells us that God made the human family as the culminating work of His creation:

Then God said, "Let us make man in our image, after our likeness. And let them have dominion over the fish of the sea and over the birds of the heavens and over the livestock and over all the earth and over every creeping thing that creeps on the earth." So God created man in his own image, in the image of God he created him; male and female he created them. And God blessed them. And God said to them, "Be fruitful and multiply and fill the earth and subdue it, and have dominion over the fish of the sea and over the birds of the heavens and over every living thing that moves on the earth." (Genesis 1:26-28 ESV)

The first thing that pops out for me in these verses is God's use of the plural when referring to Himself—"Let us." This points ahead to the reality revealed throughout the Bible, which is that God is Three in One, a dynamic community of persons that interact in complete harmony with one another. God is, in fact, a *family*—Father, Son, and Holy Spirit. So when the Bible says that God creates us "in His image," that doesn't just mean that each of us individually is a representation of God. That's what most of us mean when we say that people are "made in the image of God"—we're thinking of them as unique, separate individuals who have intrinsic value because they are human beings, and who even have a triune nature like God made of spirit, soul, and body. And that is absolutely true, but it's not the whole story. These verses are also saying that *the human family is the representation of God.*

Consider the assignment God gave to Adam and Eve—to be fruitful, multiply, fill the earth, subdue it. None of those tasks could be accomplished by one person. This is a mission for a team. God specifically emphasized this point to Adam in Genesis 2. Before God created Eve, He had Adam name all the animals so he could discover that none of the animals belonged on his team. None of the animals could be his *ezer kenegdo*, his "helpful opposite." He needed a complementary partner who was like him and yet unlike him in critical ways, so that when they came together with both their similarities and their differences, they could accomplish the mission God had given them. Finally, when animal after animal had come up short, God brought Eve to Adam and there she was! "Then the man said, 'This at last is bone of my bones and flesh of my flesh'" (Genesis 2:23 ESV). The very next verse is the one we always hear at weddings, because this moment where Adam sees Eve *was* actually their wedding, officiated by none other than God Himself, their Father: "Therefore a man shall leave his father and his mother and hold fast to his wife, and they shall become one flesh."

It is specifically this couple—not just them as individuals—that God blesses. He blesses their covenant and their connection, because it is that covenant connection that takes two separate people made in the image of God and makes them a family made in the image of God. Out of that

35

relationship, all the families of the earth, the human race, will come, and it's their covenant connection—which doesn't just bind them together, but also binds them to God and to those future generations—that will cause that family to truly represent God as they grow and fill the planet.

THE ASSIGNMENT OF FAMILY

Now this family had a job to do as God's representatives. They were supposed to get busy expanding the team, and they were to "take dominion" and "subdue" the natural world. They were not only supposed to be fruitful making babies, they were also supposed to help the whole world become fruitful by working with it and unlocking its potential. They were to expand the boundaries of the Garden where God had placed them by taming the wild, chaotic frontiers and bringing them into order and flourishing. They were to be cultivators, culture-makers.

However, there was also a very specific way they were supposed to fulfill this assignment, and that was through connection with God and each other. We know this because of the threat that soon appeared to attack them and their assignment. When the serpent tempted them to eat the fruit of the Tree of the Knowledge of Good and Evil, he enticed them to take something that was designed to come through connection with God—wisdom and knowledge to be like Him—in a way that violated their connection with Him, and thus cut them off from what they needed to fulfill their assignment.

The fact that Adam and Eve wanted knowledge and wisdom points to something important, which is that God did not create humans pre-programmed with all the knowledge and wisdom they needed to run the planet. He intended them to be always growing and learning from Him as they fulfilled their design to be His family. Because that's what happens in a family. You have kids, and then you raise them to adulthood. And you raise them through connection. Other species on the planet, especially non-mammals, pop out their offspring and those little critters are pretty much independent right away. Human beings are different. Babies come into the world totally dependent on their parents not just for their physical survival but also to develop physically, emotionally, mentally, and spiritually.

Over the last few decades, neuroscientists and psychologists have given scientific language to the process of *attachment*—the physical, emotional, mental, and social bond that forms in our brains and our children's brains as we interact with them, particularly face-to-face, and meet their needs. Establishing healthy, secure attachment between a parent and child is critical for that child to develop in every way, from physical milestones like crawling, walking, and speaking to psychosocial milestones like forming their personality and sense of self. This dynamic of secure attachment is actually how God designed His family to work, both in our human relationships and in our relationship with Him as Father. One of the dominant themes we see play out across the Bible is that God wants to be *present* with human beings—the whole story culminates with God coming to earth Himself in the form of Jesus to be Immanuel, "God with us." The Hebrew word for "presence" literally means "face." Our Father wants to connect with us face-to-face, because that is how we attach with Him—that is, form a connection—and grow up to reflect Him. As Paul put it in 2 Corinthians, "And we all, with unveiled face, beholding the glory of the Lord, are being transformed into the same image from one degree of glory to another" (2 Corinthians 3:18 ESV). We become like God—and become ourselves—through face-to-face connection with Him.

So this was God's original design for us as humans—that we would live, grow up, and fulfill our assignment to make family and make culture out of deep, face-to-face, and heart-to-heart connection with Him and each other.

THE BROKEN IMAGE

Unfortunately, Adam and Eve listened to the enemy and fell for the temptation to try to be like God outside of connection with Him, and as they soon discovered, violating their connection with God didn't just hurt that relationship—it immediately cascaded out and harmed their connections with everyone and everything else. Where before they had been comfortable with themselves in their own bodies, now they covered up to hide their shame. Where they had been united as husband and wife, now they blamed each other for their poor choices. And where they had been in harmony with the animals and the land, now their work of cultivation became a constant struggle.

This dynamic of broken connections is what we call "the curse," and this is the dynamic everyone has been living in since the Fall. Now, as Christians, we know that Jesus freed us from the curse of sin and death. But that doesn't mean we're all fully experiencing and living in that freedom. At some point in our spiritual journeys, it dawns on us that the curse of Genesis 3 isn't just still alive and well—it's actually the "normal" most of us have been swimming in our whole lives. It's what we naturally default to until we learn to fight the war of connection and go on a journey of maturity through the grace Jesus died to give us.

For me, it was some time after Ben and I had our breakthrough that I read Genesis 3:16 and realized it was talking about me during the first six years of our marriage: "And you will desire to control your husband, but he will rule over you." In essence, this verse is saying, the constant driver of disconnection between husband and wife is this fear-driven power dynamic that seeks to control and rule each other, rather than rule together as partners as we were originally designed. In our case, my attempts to grab control and responsibility away from Ben and take the power in the relationship only led to him being disempowered and me being controlled by my fear of trusting him. As long as we were both operating in this fearful dynamic, we were cut off from experiencing the kind of connection and partnership we both longed for.

The dynamics of disconnection may play out in different ways for each of us, but we all have them in our lives. We struggle in our connection with ourselves, especially our physical bodies, wrestling with insecurity and shame. We struggle in connection with others—by the time we reach adulthood, we all have stories of pain from our relationships with our parents, siblings, friends, potential mates, and others. And in marriage, we struggle in our connection with our spouse, wrestling over our needs, different personalities, and roles. As my dad says, "The two become one—and then spend the next twenty-five years fighting over which 'one.'"

At the root of these patterns of disconnection is the problem of pain. As God announced to Adam and Eve, the primary consequence of violating their connections with Him and each other was that they would now experience pain in fulfilling their unique roles and responsibilities in the family team. For the woman, pain is tied to having children, and I think that encompasses more than the physical pain of giving birth. Because we carry children inside us, in general we women feel the weight of responsibility for bringing them into the world and nurturing them much earlier and much more acutely than men. Meanwhile, men are cursed with pain in working the ground, in being the protectors and providers who must go out and battle the world to create a place where their families can live and thrive. This pain means that growing up and taking on these normal adult responsibilities has never been easy for the human race. It's not the Millennial generation or Gen Z that has suddenly begun to struggle with how to find a spouse, marry, have and raise children, and build successful careers. These are things that every generation since Adam and Eve has found uncomfortable, challenging, and intimidating—even in traditional cultures where the expectations of how people fulfill these responsibilities are much more clear or rigid.

Embracing and enduring pain to fulfill our responsibilities is one of the central aspects of what it means to grow up, but that is a response that must be learned. Since the Fall, our default setting is to react to pain or the threat of pain with fear and self-protection—fight, flight, or freeze. Most evolutionary biologists and psychologists argue that this survival instinct developed in us when we were in a primitive caveman state fighting off saber-tooth tigers. That may be true. But what Scripture shows us is that when sin entered the world, there was a profound change in human psychology. We went from being naked and unashamed to hiding and covering ourselves in fear. When God finds them in the Garden, Adam says, "I heard the sound of you in the garden, and I was afraid, because I was naked, and I hid myself" (Genesis 3:10 ESV). This is the first mention of fear in the Bible, and it didn't come because Adam and Eve encountered some monster in the woods. Fear came because they stepped out from under the protection of their connection with God. Becoming spiritually alienated and orphaned from the Father made this world a scary and painful place, and caused us to actually *devolve* back into a state where our survival brain was dominant over our attached, attuned, regulated, connected brain. According to the Bible, this is where our default to living in survival mode comes from. And we can only evolve out of survival mode and back to overcoming and thriving to the degree that we come back into trust and connection—first with God, and then with one another.

This is the whole purpose of the gospel—to restore that trust and connection, and in doing so, to restore us back to the image of God. Through His death and resurrection, Jesus broke the curse of disconnection by reconciling the Father's estranged human family back to the divine family we were originally created to be part of. Just as importantly, He sent His Holy Spirit to live inside us and make that relationship real to us. The Holy Spirit is the One who guides us into forming a *secure attachment* with the Father, convincing us we are no longer slaves to fear but deeply loved sons and daughters who have nothing to fear and cannot be separated from the love of God. He is the one "called to our side" (Gr: *paraklētos*)—the Comforter,

Intercessor, Advocate, and Helper who makes the presence of God real to us, calms our fears, infuses us with courage, and reminds us we are never alone. He is also the Spirit of unity who teaches us how to see and love one another as brothers and sisters in the family of God. This is why one of the primary things Spirit-led leaders like Peter and Paul focused on in their New Testament letters was teaching the newly formed entity called the "church" what it meant to be a family. The early church quickly became famous for bringing together people who had never socialized with each other before, much less had ever seen one another as family members. This is what the Holy Spirit does—He helps us to overcome our classic fears of other people who are different from us and leads us into a connected experience called "fellowship." The Greek word *koinonia* actually means "communion," "participation," and "partnership." The classic metaphor Paul uses for *koinonia* is the "body" of Christ. Our bodies are made up of all different, unique, yet complementary parts that must function and participate together. Separated from a body, a heart or an eye or a hand may be unique and interesting, but its purpose can never be expressed. Only when each part is joined to the others as designed can each part thrive in its individual function and cause the whole body to thrive. God's incredible design for our physical bodies is just a microcosm of His design for His family. Our Father's plan and purpose is for all of us to grow up into our full individual potential by finding our place to belong and flourish in His family.

ME, YOU, US

This same principle of God's design for our bodies and the body of Christ applies to our nuclear families. The Father's original design is that each family unit of dad, mom, and kids would function like a body made of unique and complementary parts, each playing an essential role that contributes to the health and thriving of the whole.

This has huge implications for us in understanding the overall goal of parenting. In modern Western culture, we typically imagine that successful parenting looks like raising independent, confident kids who fly the nest at the proper time and build a successful career and family of their own. But this isn't exactly the biblical picture. Yes, we want to raise healthy, confident kids with secure identities and good character. Yes, we want to equip them with a good work ethic and a covenant mindset that will prepare them to succeed in the original human assignment of making culture and making family. But in our culture, we tend to emphasize teaching our kids freedom, independence, and individuality over teaching them belonging, responsibility, and connection. We downplay teaching them to see themselves as inextricably connected to a whole, and having a crucial role to play in that whole. This is a problem because according to God's design, these two things—our individual growth into a unique self, and our critical participation in the growth and thriving of our family, the body of Christ, and the larger human family—are interdependent. We can't have one without the other.

So what is the biblical goal of parenting? Obviously we want to raise our kids to know and walk with the Lord; love Him with all their heart, soul, mind, and strength; and love their neighbors as themselves—and prepare them to overcome every obstacle thrown up by the world, the flesh, and the devil sent to deter them from that course. But to do that successfully, we need to operate with a relational paradigm that honors and protects this interdependence of individual and family growth. In God's original design, the marriage relationship comes before the parenting relationship in part, I believe, because marriage is where we should start to learn to operate in this relational paradigm. I describe this as having a "Me, You, Us" paradigm for marriage. We understand that each of us is a unique individual with our own life, personality, interests, gifts, abilities, hopes, dreams, and purpose, and that we bring those to a covenant connection where we share life together. The dance in marriage is learning to keep Me, You, and

Us in balance so that none of these three things grows out of proportion and dominates the others. Here's a basic picture of how that should look:

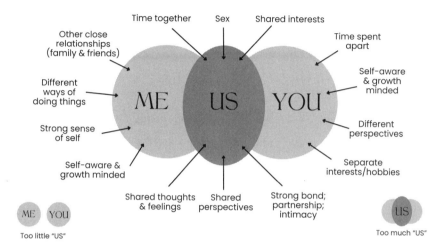

When we live out this paradigm in a healthy way, we create a living, daily example for our kids of what it looks like for two people who are so different from each other to love and serve each other, pursue and protect connection with each other, forgive and adjust when there's something hurting the connection, meet one another's needs, celebrate and encourage each other's uniqueness, and ultimately enjoy each other. This example is the reality, more than anything we could ever teach or preach at our kids, that will call and encourage them to discover and grow in their individuality while also calling them to pay attention to, love, and serve their family members.

THE CONNECTION TOOLBOX

Okay, I know the previous paragraph probably sounds pretty idealistic and even unrealistic. But we're talking about God's design, which means that even though getting there will be long, challenging, and messy, there is grace specifically designated to help us achieve that level of mature love in our marriages and our families. Our job is not to ask how and when it will happen, but again, to say yes to the Lord and to the journey.

When Ben and I began to say yes to the goal of cultivating the Me, You, Us paradigm in our marriage, God's grace showed up for us first by helping us clearly identify the two primary relational skills where we needed to grow: self-awareness and learning to understand our differences. As Stephen Covey says, "Seek first to understand, and then to be understood." That which we don't understand we do not value, and often fear. Understanding produces empathy, the ability to put ourselves in each other's shoes and view the world through each other's eyes. The view may look very different from where you're standing, but by learning to see what you see, my own vision expands and I can start to appreciate where you're coming from. Until we have self-awareness and empathetic understanding, then no matter how many sermons we may hear on how a husband and wife are supposed to complement each other, our differences are only going to be a trigger for fear, frustration, and the old controlling power dynamics. But once we gain self-awareness and understanding, we discover how our differences are gifts we can leverage to both grow and mature as individuals and to become more deeply connected as a couple than we ever imagined. And there is *nothing* that benefits our kids more than we as parents becoming mature and deeply connected. (Of course, this principle of seeking self-awareness and understanding applies to all relationships, not just in marriage. Half of being able to understand someone else is growing to understand yourself. So if you're a single parent, you need these skills too.)

Thankfully, no sooner did we start seeing where we needed to grow than we started finding the tools and resources to meet that need. As it happened, this was the season where Ben and I were both working at Bethel Church—he was in the youth department and I was in the children's department. It also happened that my dad was in charge of staff development at the time and recruited us to be part of a cohort of young leaders on staff for a leadership training program. Everyone in the program was required to complete a number of personality and behavior style assessments.

After taking them and going through our results together, the first thing these assessments did for us was to confirm and explain what we both already knew, which was that Ben and I are basically complete opposites by every measurement of personality, motivation, and behavior style. However, reading our personality and behavior style profiles together helped us finally understand that the quirks of our personalities were features, not bugs. These things that felt so strange about each other were actually baked into our design. That meant we could discover how to operate best in our personalities but we couldn't fundamentally change them. This made it even more undeniable that demanding "Be like me!" was a fruitless approach, and that it was time to start exploring the wild notion that (1) these differences were actually what attracted us to each other in the first place—because it's true, opposites *do* attract—and (2) if we truly learned to see them for what they were created to be, we could start experiencing them as gifts to help us grow and meet each other's needs.

It wasn't a mistake that the benefit of these tools really started to show up for us when we finally started to lock on to the right goal—a healthy connection—for the right reasons—loving and serving each other as true partners. When I am coaching couples one on one or teaching a workshop, I will often ask if any of them have taken an assessment like DISC or the Love languages. Most people say yes, they have. However, after a few more questions it becomes clear that they have never grabbed on to those tools and really used them to their full potential, and I suspect it's because they haven't yet found the right goal or reason. If you take a personality test purely for "personal development," you probably won't get very much out of it. Certainly, if we use the information selfishly to excuse our bad behavior or judge others, we will never attain true self-awareness. Self-awareness is actually the opposite of selfishness, because self-awareness only comes through humility and is an essential element *of* humility. In Philippians 2, Paul famously described humility as the posture of looking out for the interests of others—just as Christ looked out for our interests by laying aside His heavenly position, identifying fully with our humanity, and connecting with us so that we could ultimately identify with Him. True self-awareness comes to us as we pursue the goal of building a loving connection with the people around us, starting with our spouse and kids. This can seem counterintuitive, because most of us imagine that "dying to ourselves" or "emptying ourselves" and becoming a "servant" like Jesus means kind of rejecting or erasing ourselves and just living for others. But that's not what happened to Jesus when He humbled Himself, and it's not what happens to us. The path of humility and love is actually the only path that leads to true self-awareness, self-acceptance, and self-actualization.

As Ben and I discovered, a personality assessment done right will help you grow in self-acceptance while helping you accept each other. There's a learning curve to these tools that usually has about four or five stages. First, there's the initial curiosity—*Ooh, I want to learn more about myself!* Then apprehension—*Ack, what if this exposes things about me I don't want to accept?* Then immediate rejection—*What? That is not me!* Then the undeniability of the truth—*Okay, yes, that is me.* And then, if everyone is using the tool as it was designed, comes the best part—the part where your spouse, friend, or coworker goes, "Oh, that's why you do that thing you do. Now I get it." Their understanding and acceptance nudge you to accept yourself more fully. Eventually, if you continue to use these tools and feedback well, you start to see how your quirks, your strengths, and your weaknesses are all essential parts of you, and that instead of trying to run from or perfect the parts you don't like, you can accept the whole of who you are. Your self deserves understanding from *you* just as much as from those around you.

Whenever an "I need you to be like me!" reaction crops up in our relationships, typically it stems from insecurity in who we are. In marriage, we try to determine "which one" the two will be without seeing that neither of us knows very well who we are in the first place. Much of our self-perception is still based in a false identity full of perfectionistic expectations rather than on the revelation of who we were lovingly created to be by God. Then we turn around and project that onto our kids. Until we gain self-awareness, our "discipline" will not really be "training a child in the way they should go" and helping them to discover and live in their God-given design, but trying to fit them into our own flawed mold. But when we shift to the goal of Me, You, Us, we finally get to discover who "me" and "you" actually are. We get to be loving mirrors in which we can see our own reflection more clearly and thus be ourselves more fully.

After experiencing significant breakthroughs in our ability to understand and accept each other, Ben and I became hooked on assessments and tools and soon added more to our toolbox. Each of these tools expanded our language for understanding our personalities, behavior styles, strengths, weaknesses, core motivations, defining narratives, fears, desires, sins, and virtues. Over time, this language became ingrained in the way we communicated with each other, the way we parented our kids, the way we interacted with our friends and coworkers, and the way we led, counseled, and coached the children, youth, and eventually married couples and families we were responsible for in our ministry jobs.

So just in case you're not familiar with them, I'm going to give you a brief introduction to two of the tools we have used the most in our marriage and parenting—the five love languages and DISC. I'm not going to do any in-depth teaching or training on how to use these tools, but I want to describe them enough to show you how they have helped us understand and connect with each other more deeply. I highly encourage you to go and check them out for yourself, and I'll include some information about where you can start to do that.

THE 5 LOVE LANGUAGES

Probably one of the biggest reasons Gary Chapman's book *The 5 Love Languages* became an instant classic and is still a huge bestseller with many spin-off titles for kids, teens, singles, married couples, blended families, and more—there's even a "military edition"—is not just that the core concept is true; it's that like DISC, it's also simple to grasp and easy to remember. We only have five love languages to learn and keep track of:

- Touch
- Gifts
- Acts of Service
- Words of Affirmation
- Quality Time

The basic idea is that love can be expressed in these five basic ways, but each of us "hears" love primarily through one or two. Learning how the important people in our lives like to give and receive love is one of the important ways we can get to know them, meet their needs, and become confident that when we try to send them the message "I love you," it's going to hit the target. Hitting the target means their "love tank" will be filled and our connection will be strengthened.

You can find a free assessment to identify your primary love language or languages on Gary Chapman's site, https://5lovelanguages.com. It takes minimal time to fill out, and they give you a helpful description of each of the languages and guidance on pursuing other resources if you want to learn more.

My primary love languages are Gifts and Acts of Service. Ben's are Touch and Words of Affirmation. Once again, we are complete opposites, which means that to speak each other's love languages, we had to learn to show love in ways different to how we ourselves prefer to be loved. When we discovered this, it explained so much of why we had struggled to get and stay connected in the early years of our marriage. There I was struggling with body shame and the desire to even get close enough to touch Ben or let him touch me, and then at the end of day I would unload my frustration and criticism on him—a one-two punch that sent the clear message "I don't love you." Meanwhile, Ben was struggling with trying to figure out how to even help me with acts of service when I kept yanking all the responsibility away or criticizing him for not doing things the way I wanted him to do them. And let's just say that in those years, his attempts at getting gifts for me were . . . well, thankfully we laugh about them now.

From the moment we discovered each other's love languages and started learning how to speak them, however, our level of feeling loved and connected improved dramatically. That didn't necessarily mean it was easy. Even now that we've learned exactly how to send the "I love you" message to each other in the way we best hear it, it can still be a stretch for both of us at times because we are just so different. In my mind, touch is something I would naturally only show when it's purposeful and fitting to the occasion. In Ben's mind, touch is appropriate and meaningful in *every* situation. In my mind, we live in a home full of things that need to be washed, folded, organized, cleaned, wiped, vacuumed, put away, put together, hung up, thrown out, fed, watered, trimmed, mowed, and weeded, and I'm the one responsible to pay attention to all of them. In Ben's mind, many of these things simply wouldn't pop up as being urgent or even on his radar if he didn't know they were important to me. We don't hear love the same way at all, but we have learned to pay attention and intentionally speak one another's love language because when we do, we see the effect on each other and our connection. Operating with a full love tank is so much better than running on fumes.

It's also been fascinating to observe our children through the lens of the love languages and discover that these things are very much wired into their personalities and started showing up in the way they tried to engage with us from the time they were tiny.

Adalyn is a Gifts girl. She has always paid attention to what people liked and made presents for them. When she was still in diapers, she wrapped up my phone, put it in a tissue box, and gave it to me. As soon as she was old enough and we gave her a little bit of money, she wanted to pick out presents for people on any special occasion. I remember one Christmas when she was five years old, she bought my dad Peanut M&Ms because she had already noticed they were his favorite. She also picked out a gin cocktail book from the dollar section at Target and put it in my mom's stocking because she'd seen Mimi enjoying a gin and tonic from time to time!

Meanwhile, Delani is a Quality Time girl. When she was about ten, she drove home from church with Ben and my dad, and when they got back both men commented on how Delani had literally talked nonstop the entire half-hour drive. She had this natural urge to be fascinating and interesting to them. Coffee dates, trips to the nail salon together, and other times to connect one on one are guaranteed ways to fill Delani's love tank.

Another aspect of discovering our kids' love languages has been noticing how they are sensitive when we fail to speak to them. Following in his daddy's footsteps, Lincoln is a Words of Affirmation guy. He's also now a first-degree black belt in taekwondo, which makes me so proud! But a few years ago in his early days of training, there was one practice where he took a direct kick to the head. He shed some tears but recovered. Afterwards in the car, I asked how he was feeling. He said it had been kind of scary but had hurt only a little. I told him I was proud of him for pushing through and asked what his teachers had said. He said they told him he needed to block more. Then I said, "That kid has one impressive kick! You should practice trying to do that when we get home!" I had no idea how my words would affect his tender heart. After a few moments of silence, I heard his little teary voice ask, "Does that mean you don't like my kicks?" It was a good lesson for me that I needed to read my Words of Affirmation son a bit better before talking to him about "improvements."

DISC

One of the best things about DISC is that you only have to remember four categories: Dominance, Influence, Steadiness, and Conscientiousness. Your individual personality is a unique combination of how you score in these four categories, but when you take the assessment, the one with the highest score is where you'll find the most noticeable aspects of how you operate, show up, and "happen" in the world.

The Dominance scale measures how you relate to challenges. A high D personality is someone who loves challenges and attacks them head-on. Ds are task-driven, addicted to getting stuff done (or as my mom says, "GSD"), and need to feel like they're achieving and winning at whatever they're trying to accomplish. In their communication style they can often be very abrupt, direct, and businesslike.

The Influence scale measures how you interact with people and promote your ideas. Someone with a high I personality loves sharing their thoughts and opinions and making people feel inspired, entertained, moved, provoked, or influenced in some way. They are typically verbal processors and creative thinkers who like nothing better than a good brainstorming session or long meandering chat where they can talk about anything and everything. Is bring freedom and fun wherever they go.

The Steadiness scale measures how you relate to the pace of life and change in your environment. Those with a high S personality love to find the spots in the environment where there is the greatest need for someone dependable, someone who can bring peace and stability. Ss are the salt of the earth—loyal, supportive, dependable, and hardworking. They are people-driven like the Is, but what they love most about interacting with others is the stability that comes from building deep, low-conflict connections with people.

The Conscientiousness scale measures how you relate to rules and procedures. The high C personality is a lover of all things accurate, precise, detailed, correct, and by the book. They are task-driven like the Ds, but what they love most isn't just getting things done; it's getting them done *right*. This means they like to take their time to gather all the information they need, analyze the situation from every angle, test their theories and ideas for weak spots, and then execute when they are certain they've landed on the correct course of action.

There's lots more to say about each of these four categories, but hopefully that's enough information to help you get started with DISC. As far as I know, no one owns DISC. There are multiple organizations that have developed DISC assessments and training/coaching resources to help you understand the many facets of your profile and how to use this information for personal growth and for interacting with others more effectively, so I recommend that you explore and find the one that fits you best.

So surprise, surprise—I have a high D personality. When I learned my DISC profile, I finally understood why I had always wanted to work at least part time even after I started having babies. I had a driving urge to get stuff done and feel like I was winning. It was my personality, not a character flaw. That didn't mean I didn't have rough edges to my D that needed to be softened—of course I did, and still do. While many aspects of our personality are fixed, our level of maturity is not fixed, and the point of learning DISC, or any personality typing system, is to discover the path of growth we must take to mature in our personality so that who we are becomes a gift to those around us. For me, that path started with understanding that my strong desire to achieve was an expression of my core design, and that design was good. I just had to learn how to pursue that desire in a way that inspired and blessed others rather than intimidated them.

Where DISC probably helped Ben and me most was in our approach to conflict. As a high D, I am naturally direct, comfortable with confrontation, and eager to address and resolve issues quickly rather than walking by them each day and not doing anything. As a high S, Ben is naturally conflict avoidant and loves to take his time before getting around to addressing issues.[3] Before understanding these aspects of our personality, I saw Ben as irresponsible and frustrating, and he saw me as scary and dominating. But after we cultivated an appreciation for what each other needs—I need to know that problems are going to be addressed and solved, and he needs to know that our connection is going to be okay in the process—we both learned to adjust our approach to conflict so that we lower each other's anxiety and lean into the conversations we need to have.

Funny enough, none of our kids have high D personalities. Delani was feisty and willful as a child, and was always pushing my buttons and boundaries, but as she's grown up it's become clear that she's highest on the S scale, like Ben. Adalyn's and Lincoln's personalities are still emerging, but so far Adalyn has displayed many traits high on the I and C scales, and Lincoln's tender heart and deep value for the relationships closest to him suggest that he will be high on the S scale.

One of the classic scenarios where this difference in our personalities has played out is at bedtime. When I put the kids to bed, I am focused on accomplishing the task of getting the kids in their pajamas with their teeth brushed at a proper time. I tuck them into bed, snuggle with them for a bit, and then kiss them goodnight. When Ben puts the kids to bed, it is literally a completely different story. He will disappear in their rooms for over an hour to talk to them about their days, read them books, or make up elaborate stories about dragons, knights, and princesses. I don't know how many nights he has regaled them with the fantastic tale of three guinea pigs named "Bebani," "Baddy" and "Babincoln" who escaped in the house and had adventures. For the Ss in the family, bedtime has always been about connection, not the task of going to bed. And they *love* it.

---

[3] More specifically, if you are familiar with DISC, I'm a DC and Ben is an IS.

TOOLS GIVE LANGUAGE

As I hope you can see, the great benefit of learning to use DISC and the love languages is that they give you descriptive language to see and appreciate one another's behavior and personality. There is so much power in being able to give names to the nuances of how we experience each other and ourselves. I imagine this is why God assigned Adam to name the animals—because in the process of observing each unique animal and giving language to their behavior, he also came to understand himself, and immediately recognized Eve as his counterpart when God brought her to him.

Sadly, so many couples never really invest the time and effort in developing the relational language, intelligence, and skills necessary to know and understand themselves and each other on this deep level. As my dad often jokes, he knows guys who have studied more about the intricacies of bass fishing than they have about their own wives. I'm sure the same can be said of wives who devote more time to understanding their kids or jobs or even the Bible rather than their husbands. It is easier to get a PhD in psychology than it is to actually come to know yourself and another human being deeply, because the PhD doesn't require the same level of emotional vulnerability, humility, trust, and commitment to growth. But studying bass fishing, psychology, or even the Bible can't provide our hearts with what we most deeply desire and need, and what our kids most need from us as their parents, which is to live in a marriage and family of deep, healthy connection. This is what we were created for. Every investment and sacrifice we make on the journey to master connection is worth it.

4

The Structure of Connection: Love

YOU'VE PROBABLY BEEN WONDERING WHEN we're going to get to the practical part of this book and start looking at some actual parenting tools. Well, good news—over the next five chapters, we're going to explore a lot of tools. But over many years of coaching parents, I've seen time and again that giving people tools without laying enough groundwork for them to understand the overall goal of becoming an imperfect but engaged parent often leads to them misusing the tools, and then concluding they don't work. Engaged parenting isn't a set of techniques—it's a philosophy and a culture rooted in the biblical principles of operating from love instead of fear, from vision and purpose instead of reactive survival mode, and from fighting to protect "us" instead of protecting myself. The tools and techniques of engaged parenting only make sense in that broader context, which will become more and more evident (I hope) as our parenting story continues and we now start to dive into them.

THE SEVEN PILLARS

About four years after Ben and I got really intentional about working on our connection and building our skills of self-awareness and understanding, we experienced another season where we were challenged to become even more intentional about the culture we were building in our family. When we moved from Redding to Sacramento in 2013 to help plant the Jesus Culture Sacramento church, we left the Bethel Church community where we had lived, worked, and built relationships for over a decade. Delani was eight by this point, Adalyn was four, and Lincoln was two. The girls had only gone to Bethel Christian School. Our friends were mostly colleagues on staff at the church. We had been absolutely immersed in and riding on the momentum of this beautiful and strong culture and community that we certainly appreciated, enjoyed, and believed in, but which was also the only culture we really knew.

When we moved to Sacramento, many things we had taken for granted were now gone. We were both leading in various capacities at Jesus Culture Sacramento and at Loving on Purpose, which was great, but everything was new and needed to be built, so our roles and responsibilities looked different and we didn't have the same support and resources we had in our previous jobs, church, and community. Some familiar faces from Bethel had moved down with the church planting team, but there were also plenty of new people, so it felt like our community had shrunk dramatically. There was no Christian school, so we had to put our kids in public schools. Ben also started studying at university to earn his bachelor's in social work, which was another new environment and culture to navigate.

Basically, Ben and I got to see a very valuable, though initially uncomfortable, truth. In Redding, we had been relying on the wider Bethel culture and community to lead, teach, and support us and our kids in the values and practices we believed in much more than we realized. With those gone or greatly diminished in Sacramento, it revealed that our ability to lead in creating that culture was not at the level we thought. We soon recognized that if we were going to succeed in this new place and season of life, we needed to increase our level of ownership over what we were intentionally choosing and cultivating in our marriage and home, no matter what anyone else was doing around us.

So we started asking ourselves some really important questions. Who were the Serpells apart from Bethel, from Jesus Culture, and even from Loving on Purpose and the Silks? What were the things we wanted to protect in our home, and how were we going to model that for our kids? How were we going to create not just healthy connections but also a culture in our home that would train our kids with the tools and character to be Serpells at school, at sports practice, at youth group, with their friends, with potential boyfriends and girlfriends, and ultimately as they launched out of our home?

Once again, being in leadership roles created some extra urgency for us to start finding answers to these questions. Everyone around us was leaning on us to give them strength and wisdom on how to build healthy marriages and families, and we knew we couldn't give away what we didn't have ourselves. Thankfully, of course, we weren't starting from scratch—along with our growing understanding of God's design for relationships and family, DISC, the love languages, and other assessments, we had plenty of tools, wisdom, and resources to draw from, many of which we were already using. We just had to get a clearer vision of the family culture we were building so we could use them more consistently and effectively.

As it happened, my dad's book *Keep Your Love On* came out right around the time we moved to Sacramento. I had heard him teach the material in the book for years, and had been teaching many of the concepts myself as a leader in Bethel's children's ministry, but now we became immersed in it and began using and recommending it as a resource to everyone we were coaching and leading. The whole book is amazing—it's the kind of book you want to read and reread because it brings you back to the principles that must ground you as you battle in the war of connection. But there was one particular chapter in *Keep Your Love On* that Ben and I both grabbed on to as a template for the family culture we were wanting to build. The chapter focuses on a concept my dad developed called "The Seven Pillars of Healthy Relationships," inspired by Proverbs 9:1: "Wisdom has built her house; she has set up its seven pillars" (NIV). I had been teaching the Seven Pillars at Bethel, but when the book came out, we had this sense of conviction, like, "Yes, that is our vision for the qualities and character traits we wanted to cultivate in our marriage, in our kids, and in our home." God's design for family (unique, individual parts thriving and growing through a vital connection to the whole) had given us our overall goal of connection and becoming a whole, healthy family, but the Seven Pillars gave us a way to describe and measure what growth and success in achieving that goal looked like. The Seven Pillars are:

1 Love
2 Honor
3 Trust
4 Responsibility
5 Self-Control
6 Vision
7 Faith

One of the things I had already begun to discover in teaching the Seven Pillars in the children's ministry was that this framework anchored all the marriage and parenting tools we had been using and teaching over the years. The personality tests, love languages, Love and Logic—all of these show us *how* to build healthy connections and culture in our homes. But the Seven Pillars tell us exactly *what* we are building with these tools and *why*. Again, over the years I have seen many people try to use parenting tools without having a grasp on the *why*, and it doesn't exactly work out for them. So over the next five chapters, I'm going to guide you through each of the Seven Pillars, show you what Ben and I have been doing to cultivate them, and explain how the parenting tools should function in this framework. In this chapter, we'll focus on the first pillar—love.

LOVE: A SAFE CONNECTION

Love is the first of the Seven Pillars, but it's also the foundation of the whole structure of connection, because the quality of love is that you feel connected heart to heart. In infancy and early childhood, we lay the foundation for connection with our kids by attuning to their needs and doing all the things—from feeding them to changing their diapers, holding them, giving them lots of smiles and face-to-face interaction, comforting them, playing with them, etc.—that help them form a secure attachment with us as their primary caregivers. As their personalities and verbal and physical skills develop and we continue to respond to them with high levels of attunement, particularly showing that we are cued in to their internal world of thoughts, feelings, and needs, their attachment with us gradually evolves into a genuine heart-to-heart connection—not only with us, but also with their siblings and other important relationships.

There is probably nothing more gratifying or delightful as a parent than to see our kids learning to love and thrive in their connections with us and others. One of my absolute favorite moments of seeing the pillar of love on display in our home took place at Christmas a few years ago. As I mentioned in the last chapter, Adalyn has a Gifts love language that shows up in her ability to give gifts that really hit the target with the "I love you" message. In the month or so leading up to this particular Christmas, she began begging me to help her buy a certain T-shirt for Lincoln that had the word "Unspeakable" printed on it in a funny font—apparently it was connected to some YouTuber I had never heard of before. I went ahead and punched in my credit card info for her, then watched in amusement as she waited with great anticipation for this shirt to arrive in the mail. On Christmas morning, our whole family gathered in the living room to open presents one at a time, starting with the youngest. Lincoln selected his gift from Adalyn as the first present to open. He ripped off the paper, held up the shirt, put it back down in his lap, and then threw his arms around his sister and burst into tears. We were all stunned at this display, but then as Lincoln continued to sob and cling to Adalyn, some of us began to brush back tears as we realized that she had clearly bought her brother a gift that was an absolute home run to his heart. Then we all started laughing, because how could anyone top that? Unless there was a puppy hiding in one of the packages under the tree, Adalyn had already beaten us all for picking the best present that Christmas morning.

Moments like these demonstrate why the love languages are the first tool we turn to for strengthening heart-to-heart connection and building the pillar of love in our home. Speaking in one another's love languages is the most direct way to make people feel seen, heard, and valued. This is why each member of our family knows what the love languages are and knows each other's love languages. We talk about them and pay attention to how we are sending the message of love back and forth to each person in the way they need to hear it.

We have also been learning that *not* speaking one another's love languages can create disconnection. For example, I used to get frustrated with Adalyn when she would come to me and ask for my help with things that I knew she could handle on her own—"Mom, can you make me a sandwich?"—or when the timing was really not ideal—"Mom, can you straighten my hair?" (fifteen minutes before we have to leave for youth group). But over time, I started to notice that whenever I brushed her off or denied her request, she would become sad and discouraged, whereas when I did what she was asking, she rewarded me with effusive gratitude. Eventually it dawned on me that after Gifts, Acts of Service was probably Adalyn's secondary love language. Asking for my help was really a bid for connection with me, so when I regularly turned her down, I was creating some disconnection between us. As soon as I realized this, I became much more attentive to how I was responding in these moments. If I couldn't help her right away, I was careful not to outright reject her request but to promise to help later at a better time.

Not speaking each other's love languages isn't the only cause of disconnection, of course. Connection is like a plant that must be nurtured, which means it can be harmed either through neglect and through direct injury. The two biggest reasons we neglect connection these days are busyness and distraction, and these seem to be pretty universal with every family I know. When we're not running around from dawn to dusk with our impossible to-do lists, we're zoning out to social media or entertainment on our phones or screens. Both of these starve connection, which requires *time* and *being present*.

As for direct injuries to connection, most of these happen through disrespectful communication, which we'll focus on more with the next pillar in Chapter 5. But what really drives disconnection is fear. Perfect love casts out fear, which is why love is a safe place. In a genuine loving connection, we feel safe to show up and be seen and vulnerable, and safe to struggle and fail and make mistakes without the threat of punishment. But when fear gets to be loud in our homes, it drives that experience of a safe, loving connection away. So as parents, we should be consistently asking ourselves, "Is fear my counselor? Is fear the voice I'm allowing to influence me and in turn using to influence my kids to listen and obey?"

PERFECTIONISM IN THE TRENCHES

Let's be honest—that voice of fear shows up very early in the parenting journey. For some of us, we start worrying about our kids when they're still in the womb. Certainly when that tiny infant is placed in our arms and we understand that its survival completely depends on us, most of us feel a mix of fierce love as well as terror. And then we enter the survival exercise that is caring for that child, complete with sleep deprivation and a nervous system constantly on high alert to their cries and needs. This only escalates as the child becomes mobile and enters toddlerhood, which I call "the trenches." The trenches are where these precious little humans start to introduce *mess* into our lives on a grand scale. They are messy because they are *learning*, but it's so easy to forget that and get triggered and distracted by the mess, which we of course have to clean up until they learn to do it themselves.

The toddler trenches are usually where perfectionism really starts to rear its head, because perfectionism hates mess. Perfectionism *fears* mess, because it sees it not as a necessary part of the positive process of learning but as a cause for shame and punishment. And unfortunately, that is exactly what most of us learned growing up as we made our own messes, probably starting in our own toddler years. And now that we're in survival mode with our own kids, we will inevitably fall back on that old programming unless we start to recognize the voice of fear and perfectionism and choose to shift our allegiance and obedience to the voice of love. If we don't make that shift, we will end up reacting to our child's messes with fear, shame, and punishment, which will make an even bigger mess in our relationship by removing safety from our connection. It will also simply perpetuate the cycle and teach our children that their messes are to be feared and punished rather than essential to their learning process.

I made these fear-driven messes for many years with my kids, and for a long time I wasn't great at quickly cleaning them up. One of the most important ways we can measure our own growth in building the pillar of love in our relationships is to look at how quickly and how well we clean up the messes we make when we react out of fear and perfectionism. In my early years of parenting, I would get triggered by the latest scene of destruction I had stumbled upon, unleash an angry outburst, simmer down a little and start to feel terrible, offer an apology to my child that was really an excuse, and then just kind of roll on until genuine conviction set in, sometimes days later, when I would finally try to repair the damaged connection. But over time, I got better at learning to respond instead of react (we'll talk more about this when we cover the pillar of responsibility), so those out-bursts got fewer and farther between. And when I did react, I got quicker and quicker at recognizing it, owning it, and restoring connection.

One incident stands out in my mind as the moment I knew I was really learning to clean up my messes. We had just moved to Sacramento and were living in a rental with an unfinished pool in the backyard, which meant I had to keep Lincoln, who was barely three at the time, in the house with me during the day so he wouldn't somehow wander out and fall into it.

One day I got busy making lunch, and when I went to find Lincoln, he was not where I had left him.

"Lincoln!" No answer. *Please tell me he did not manage to get outside in the backyard.*

I immediately began stalking through the rooms of the house, calling his name. When I entered the master bedroom, a strange sight met my eyes. A dark handprint, surrounded by other dark streaks of color, decorated the wall behind my bed in a kind of tribal design. Walking around the bed, I found Lincoln sitting with my fifty-dollar palette of smoky eyeshadow open on the ground before him, the applicator clutched in his fist. The wall was not the only canvas he had been working on—his face was also covered with black, navy, and gray streaks like war paint. Clumps of pigment were smeared on his hands and clothes, and also appeared to be ground into the light-colored carpet.

I'm sorry to say that all I could think about at that moment was the mess and what it would cost to clean it up. A new eyeshadow palette, carpet cleaning, wall cleaning, painting the wall, explaining it to the landlord . . . as the list began to add up in my head, I caved in to the panic.

"Lincoln! What have you done?!"

His little smudged face looked up in shock at my angry tone, his eyes widening at the sight of me bearing down on him.

"How could you do this? Look at the carpet! What did you do? *What did you do?*"

He started to cry, but I was unmoved. I picked him up, carried him into the bathroom, and turned on the shower. Without waiting for the water to get fully warm, I set him down under the stream fully clothed. I didn't want him getting makeup anywhere else. "Stay in there until I come back," I ordered.

I returned to the bedroom to survey the damage. It looked pretty bad— the carpet in particular looked like it might be permanently stained. Then, just as quickly as it had intensified, my anger began to wane, and suddenly I could hear my son wailing in the bathroom.

Oh no. The reality of what I had just done hit me in full force. *I just screamed at my son and left him in the shower. Fully clothed. Over makeup. Now he's sobbing in the other room, terrified of me.*

I walked back into the bathroom and found Lincoln huddled in the shower, cowering away from me. Instantly, my heart broke. I got on my knees, crawled into the shower, turned off the water, put my arms around him, and began to weep.

"I'm so sorry, Lincoln," I said, my voice breaking. "Mommy shouldn't have done that."

I continued to soothe Lincoln as I bathed and dressed him, and spent the rest of the day intentionally staying close to him and showing him affection. Then, after putting him to bed that night, I did what was probably the hardest thing for me, but which I knew I had to do: I forgave myself. Otherwise I knew what would happen—shame would be my counselor instead of love. I had let that happen too many times to count, and I knew it only perpetuated a perfectionistic fear of mess, and out-of-control, punishing reactions to it. Yes, the day's events had proven that fear was still in there, waiting to be triggered. But it had also proven that my goal with my son truly was connection, because the moment I had realized that I had hurt our connection by listening to fear, I had shifted immediately into repentance, restoration, and moving toward him in love.

CONNECTION IS A TWO-WAY STREET

Along with leaning into these moments of repair, one of the most crucial things we can do as parents to create and restore safety in our connection with our kids is to invite them to give us feedback about how they're experiencing us. I've had many moms come to me for coaching and shed tears as they confess, "I am Angry Mommy. That is my name." After I explain to them that this does not have to be their identity, and that their true identity is to be a daughter who gets to receive Father's love for herself and then give it to her kids, I suggest that they start checking in with their kids at the end of the day and ask, "Hey, how did Mommy do today? Was I Angry Mommy, or did I do a better job today?" If the children say, "You were a little angry, Mommy," then all they have to do is clean it up. "I'm sorry I let my angry out. I want to do better tomorrow. I love you. Thanks for telling me." Inviting our children's feedback does not mean we stop being the adult in the relationship or put undue weight of responsibility on them before they are ready to handle it. Even as we ask for it, we must also filter it and train them to give feedback effectively. But it's our job to teach them how to have a voice in our relationship. In a healthy relationship, connection and influence are a two-way street—even between a parent and child. It can be very humbling to ask a child, "Was I a nice person today?" because we know they're going to be honest. But we also know that it will be the truth spoken in love, because that is the beauty of a child—they are naturally wired for connection and love, and will freely give back to us what they receive.

Just recently, I took the kids and our dog stand-up-paddle-boarding and got flustered when Delani accidentally inflated the seventy-dollar

65

emergency life vest we had borrowed from a friend for the trip, rendering it useless. Soon, my irritation spilled over into chastising her for not being more helpful and engaged as I was struggling to wrangle everybody and the boards on the water. When we returned home, Delani disappeared into her room and I had a chance to reflect on how I had treated her. As Adalyn had witnessed the whole interaction, I asked her, "Was I too hard on Delani?"

"You were a little hard on her," Adalyn said honestly. "I don't think she meant to do that with the life jacket. You got mad at her for an accident."

So I took this feedback, went up and found Delani in her bed under the covers, laid down beside her, and said, "I blew it." After she had shed some tears and we talked through what had happened, I asked her, "What do you need from me?"—one of the most common ways we ask for feedback in our family. Ben and I do this with our kids not just because we want them to feel safe to tell Mommy and Daddy the truth but because we are modeling the behavior we want and need from them when it's our turn to give them feedback.

Parenting is called "parenting" and not "childing" because every behavior we need to address or cultivate in our kids begins with what we are modeling for them. Modeling humility with our kids is also how we teach them to do the same when they make messes and start to learn how to clean them up. Telling a child, "Say sorry to your brother," may produce compliance, but it's when they see Mommy and Daddy saying, "I'm sorry," to each other or to them that they have something to imitate, which is how they start to understand why we apologize and repair connection. Modeling cleaning up our messes with our kids also helps to remove fear around that process for our kids, and makes it clear that our goal when they mess up is not to punish them or even to get them to go through the motions of an apology or repentance but to truly learn what they need to learn from the experience. We believe in their ability to learn, just as we are learning. In fact, we know that they are geniuses who are completely capable of learning anything and everything they need to manage their end of connection with us.

We had a friend, a single woman, who started caring for a twelve-year-old boy after his mother disappeared. After quite some time passed and she hadn't returned, she got the courts involved and finally adopted him at the age of twelve. Things were going well in their relationship until the boy began to have explosive fits of rage where he would yell, slam doors, and become scary and volatile. After several incidents, this new single mom told her new son, "I need you to come up with a better plan for what you're going to do with your anger that doesn't involve becoming scary and hurting our connection." The boy retorted, "I need you to come up with a plan for how you're not going to make me angry."

So this friend decided to call in the troops. She asked us if her son could come over to our house and hang out while he worked on this anger management plan. We agreed, and when he arrived, we gave him some sunscreen and gloves, fed him lunch, and put him to work pulling weeds on our property. After an hour or two, he came to us and said he had come up with a plan, so we let him call his mom and explain it to her. She replied that they had already tried what he was suggesting multiple times and it hadn't worked, so he needed to go back to the drawing board and come up with something else. So he returned to weeding, and this time Ben and I both engaged him in conversation and started asking him some questions. "What is your mom's experience with you? How do you think your mom experiences that behavior? How's that protecting your relationship? What do you think your mom needs from you?"

Finally, after six hours of weeding and pondering, he came in and called his mom again. He explained that he realized he was an internal processor and she was an external processor, and he often felt bombarded and overwhelmed when he didn't have the time or space to think and process in their communication. He suggested that they have a code word he could use when he was starting to feel this way during a conversation, and that this meant he had permission to go to his room and take some time and space, but that later they would finish the conversation. She agreed to this plan, and as far as I know he has never had a scary outburst again. Kids really are geniuses when we invite them to be and don't get in the way of their learning!

OFFERING EMPATHY

One of our greatest responsibilities as parents is creating a safe place for our kids to learn, and that safety only comes through connection. Today, we see extremes in parenting when it comes to the issue of safety. Some parents err on the side of coddling their children too much, out of the misguided but understandable desire to protect them from experiencing anything uncomfortable, disturbing, or difficult. Others send their kids off into environments, both offline and online, where they become exposed to dangerous ideas and influences. Engaged parents, however, understand that all learning involves mess, struggle, and hard work, which is uncomfortable but necessary, and ultimately rewarding. Wisdom and character, like pearls and diamonds, are formed through pain and pressure. A child's transformation into a free, responsible, mature adult, like a caterpillar's transformation into a butterfly, only comes as it struggles to emerge from the cocoon. Our goal is to influence and encourage our kids to struggle effectively and ultimately discover the rewards of learning, growth, and character formation, and we do that not by taking away the challenge or sending them off to face it alone but by being present and connected with them as they take it on. This is just how God engages with us. He doesn't remove us from the trials and tests that are necessary for our maturity— He promises to be with us as we endure them, and encourages us along the way.

One of the primary ways we do this is by offering empathy and encouragement in their struggle. I realize that "empathy" is a tricky word for some, because just like safety, we have all seen extremes. We've seen cases where empathy is lacking in a parent's interaction—the child's thoughts, feelings, and needs are completely disregarded or even mocked. On the other extreme, there are parents who over-identify with their child's emotional state so much that they will just sit and swim in it with their kid. I've had parents come to me and describe these elaborate exchanges where they believe they are being empathetic and affirming what their child is feeling, but the child ends up exploiting the opportunity to be out of control, disrespectful, and willful in getting their way, which shows that they're obviously not learning what they need to learn.

So let me be clear—empathy doesn't mean either dissociating from or becoming a doormat for your child's emotions. Empathy does not mean removing boundaries, consequences, or discipline—quite the opposite. Empathy is the ability to read and understand what someone is thinking, feeling, and needing, and respond to that in a safe, connected, and respectful way. Our goal in showing empathy is to guide our children in their ability to understand what's going on inside them and to respond to it well, rather than reacting to it. "Yes, this is tough. Gosh, that sounds painful. I know. But I believe in you. You're going to get there. You can figure this out. You're going to make it." When our child's emotional reaction becomes disrespectful, we confront it and set boundaries. "I know you're upset and angry. That doesn't give you permission to speak to me that way. I'll be happy to continue this conversation when your voice sounds like mine." Speaking of respect—that's what we're going to be looking at in depth in the next chapter on the pillar of honor!

So this is the pillar of love—building, strengthening, and protecting heart-to-heart connection with our kids where they feel known and safe to learn and grow. We do this by:

- Speaking love languages
- Paying attention to how loud the voice of fear is
- Cleaning up our messes when we react out of fear of mess

- Asking for feedback
- Staying connected with our kids through empathy and encouragement in their learning process

Showing our kids that we can create and protect a connection that is a safe place for learning—both our learning and theirs—is the direct path to what we crave most for our kids, which is that even as they grow up, become independent, and launch into adulthood, they stay connected with us heart to heart. My personal goal is that after God Himself, my kids would trust Ben and me with their most vulnerable secrets because they see us as the safest place for their hearts.

5

The Structure of Connection: Honor

I RETURNED HOME ONE AFTERNOON to find the house empty. As I came into the kitchen, I instantly noticed something that had not been there in the morning when I left: several large divots cut into the wood of one of the cabinets near the dishwasher.

What in the world?

Investigating, I soon pulled open the cutlery drawer and found several sharp knives, one of which had a number of large scores and chunks cut out of its handle.

My suspicions immediately flew to one person: Lincoln. Before I left the house that morning, I had reminded him that he needed to unload and reload the dishwasher before he went out with Ben to get a haircut. He had tried to dodge this responsibility by going to Ben and making a case for why they ought to be leaving the house earlier so they could do a bunch of other important things on their outing. When Ben brought the case to me, I said I was fine with Lincoln doing everything on his list—he just also needed to do the dishes before he left the house.

Apparently Lincoln had not been happy with me countering his dodge. Or at least, that was my best guess, because it seemed plain that he had decided to take out his frustration with several kitchen knives. Yikes.

Thankfully, with the house to myself, I had some time and space to contemplate how I wanted to respond to this very scary and disrespectful choice my nine-year-old son had made. I considered my options. I could go into lecture mode and give him a sermon on being respectful of other people's property. I could also make him pay to repair the damaged cupboards and replace the knives. But I knew this had to be a heart issue because it was so out of character for Lincoln. I had never seen him take his anger and frustration out so destructively, so I knew that's where I needed to start the conversation.

When Lincoln got home, I called him to the kitchen, showed him the knives and cupboard, and said, "Buddy, I don't know what happened here. It feels like maybe you were upset and you chose to let that make decisions for you."

The look on his face clearly told me he knew he had made a big mess. "Yeah, I was mad at you," he admitted.

"So how does being mad at me and destroying things in our house work out for you?"

"Probably not very well."

"It's sad that you didn't decide to manage your 'mad at me,' and made a mess. I love you and this is not fun for me. Do you think you can handle it differently next time? I don't want to do this again."

"Okay," he nodded.

"I trust you," I assured him. "And I trust that you are going to learn and not do this again. But I'm also not the only one who helps pay for this house. There are three other people who pay for this house, and your choice to take out your anger toward me by destroying something has created messes with all of them. What are you going to do about it?"

"I don't know." Now he looked truly distressed.

"Well, I think you need to go to them and find out what they need from you to clean up this mess. And no Nintendo Switch until you have a plan for doing that."

So Lincoln spent the rest of the evening going to Ben, my dad, and my mom, explaining what he had done and asking them how to clean up his mess with them. Thankfully, I trusted all those people to speak to my son with the same goal of helping him take ownership not only of his actions but also of his heart.

My dad asked Lincoln if he could or could not be trusted with knives—a weighty question for Lincoln, as he had a pocket knife he loved and used to whittle sticks. They discussed this question, with my dad nudging Lincoln to prove he knew what was required to be trusted around knives, until Lincoln agreed that going forward, he was going to protect everyone in the family, and our property, in the way he handled knives.

Ben also discussed the behavior required for Lincoln to have access to knives, and then turned the focus to Lincoln's heart toward me. He explained that Lincoln's attempt to get around doing his chores, and his choice to take out his frustration and anger toward me in the way he did, felt really yucky and disrespectful. He told Lincoln he needed him to work on protecting his relationship with me, and helped him recognize how much damage it caused when he didn't.

Finally, Lincoln got to my mom. She took him to the Home Depot website, where they found wood stain pens and other products to fix the cabinet and knives, which Lincoln used his allowance to pay for. My mom also talked to him about secondary emotions. For example, anger is usually a mask for fear—fear of loss or punishment. When we let those be in charge of our body and rule what's going on, we go into a fight or flight reaction, which is often destructive and disrespectful, and never really understand why we're doing what we're doing. She asked him questions about what was really going on in his heart that led him to make those destructive choices. What was he really needing in that moment? Did he communicate those things?

By the time the knives and cupboards had been restored, my son had received an incredible lesson—not just from me, but from all his elders in the family—on what a powerful impact his choices to respond or react to strong emotions had on his important relationships, his opportunities, his time, his emotions, and even his limited money. He learned that disrespecting someone's property disrespects them, and so both the property and the relationship need to be restored to clean up the mess. It was a time-consuming process for all of us, but I'm so thankful none of us tried to speed it up or let him out of it too early, because it would only have undercut the lesson. To this day, he has never done anything like that again, and I don't think he will. He also still has access to knives, now with the awareness of what he needs to do to keep that access. In short, my son learned a vital lesson about the power of *honor* and *dishonor*.

HONOR AND PARENTING STYLES

Honor is the second of the Seven Pillars. Honor flows from the value I carry for God, myself, and others and our relationships. It is based in my ability to see each person for who they truly are, both in their universal value as a human being created in the image of God, and in their unique design as a person with a different personality, likes and dislikes, needs and wants, thoughts and feelings, talents and abilities.

Respectful behavior is the primary expression of honor. Every parent I know wants their children to be respectful (especially to them). For many parents, there's no greater trigger for anger and frustration than disrespectful behavior. We call disrespect the "big red button," and it can seem that once a child achieves a certain level of verbal skill, physical autonomy, and willfulness—certainly by the toddler stage—they have no other goal than to find our big red button and press it repeatedly.

Responding to disrespectful behavior is probably where I see parents diverge most drastically in their parenting styles. For many parents, disrespect triggers their authoritarian tendencies. Lincoln, Delani, and I witnessed a clear example of this one day at Lincoln's taekwondo studio. As we were waiting to speak to his instructor, we watched the father of one of Lincoln's classmates impatiently waiting for his son to get ready to leave. He didn't say anything, but the look on his face spoke volumes, transforming from obvious frustration to silent rage as the seconds ticked by. Finally, the man walked over to his son, grabbed his ear, and began to whisper. The only words I caught were "I told you," but the child's face wincing in pain and panic showed the intent of the message. We then watched as the boy got down and began to do pushups. At one point, the father grabbed his son's head to correct his poor form.

By now, Lincoln was looking at me with concern, as though he hoped I could do something. "That doesn't look like a very fun relationship does it?" I asked quietly.

"I wonder if that's why he's always so mean to other people when he spars with them," Lincoln whispered back insightfully. "His daddy's kind of mean."

"I think you're probably right, son," I nodded. "So sad."

We continued waiting, and eventually the father and son passed us and left the studio. After chatting with Lincoln's instructor, we also left. As soon as we got in the car, Delani launched into passionate commentary about the scene we had observed. One thing she said struck me as particularly heartbreaking: "If that dad is willing to do that in front of a whole room of people, what the heck happens at home when no one is looking?!"

Though I've never encountered this father and son outside the studio and have no idea what their life is like at home, what I know is that this father wants to be respected by his son, but he's chosen the road of fear and punishment to achieve it. As a result, he may have moments where his son displays respectful behavior, but there is likely very little honor in this relationship.

On the other hand, I see many parents reacting to their child's disrespect with permissive parenting, which is just as unhelpful when it comes to teaching honor. These situations often look like a hostage—the parent—negotiating with a terrorist—the child. I once coached one mother whose ten-year-old son was basically the tyrant of the family. This compassionate mom understood that her son, who was the fourth of her six children, was struggling with insecurities and the desire to be accepted and included by his siblings. The problem was that he was acting out his feelings of fear and anger in inappropriate and destructive ways. And instead of setting boundaries and requiring him to change his behavior, this mom just kept asking the family to accept the boy's apologies and allow him to join the rest of the family for videogames—even though last time he broke the controller in a fit of rage—or for dinner—even though the last time he threw his mashed potatoes at the wall, and on and on. Her desire to protect her son from feeling rejected was sabotaging her responsibilities to protect the rest of her family from his bad behavior and to teach her son to manage his emotions and behavior with respect and honor. This was understandably creating a less-than-honoring environment.

In recent years, "Gentle parenting" is another parenting style that has grown in popularity. Gentle parenting purports to be an authoritative or engaged style that blends a focus on connection and empathy with healthy boundaries. It has a very idealistic and noble goal, which is to train children to be emotionally aware and intrinsically motivated rather than externally motivated through rewards and punishments. While I love this in theory, in practice I have yet to see a parent who practices gentle parenting produce a child who is honoring. Instead, what I see are parents attempting to address disruptive or disrespectful behavior in the moment by asking questions, making comments, or even engaging in long conversations with the child where they discuss the child's feelings, motivations, and "unmet needs," but don't actually get the child to stop the behavior or clean up their mess. For example, one dad recently narrated a scenario in which he informed his four-year-old daughter that it was time to leave the swimming pool and go home, which prompted a meltdown tantrum. This father pulled his daughter aside and spent over thirty minutes speaking to her about her feelings, telling her he understood why she was upset, trying to get her to understand why they needed to go home, and trying to find positive things she could focus on and look forward to instead. Though he felt that the conversation was meaningful and she seemed to understand, he admitted to me that she had thrown other tantrums since then. It seemed she was taking his approach as permission to continue her behavior rather than a boundary requiring her to curtail it.

While I am all for leading with empathy, honoring my child's feelings, helping them understand their emotions, and acknowledging their needs—as was hopefully evident in the episode of Lincoln and the knives—it is critical to do this in a way that doesn't downplay or undercut the equally important message that certain behavior is disrespectful and unacceptable, and that it creates messes that must be cleaned up. Unfortunately, what I see in most cases of kids being raised with gentle parenting is that they are not really getting a clear message about what behavior is disrespectful. I suspect that the reason for this is similar to the reason parents use permissive parenting—the gentle parent is afraid to set boundaries and introduce consequences because they don't want to be authoritarian and get their child to change their behavior out of fear. This is obviously self-contradictory—we can't prevent a child from being afraid when fear is our motive for doing so. And while we can avoid punishing a child's disrespectful behavior at home, the reality is that we live in a world of rewards and punishments and at some point they will experience this. We also can't teach our children to be intrinsically motivated without also teaching them the external consequences of their behavior, both positive and negative. Obviously our ultimate goal is for them to be motivated to pursue the true and lasting reward of deep, healthy heart-to-heart connection with us, God, their siblings, and others and to want to avoid the true punishment of disconnection and isolation. But to get to that experience, we often have to introduce lesser but effective rewards and punishments—from fruit snacks and timeouts in toddlerhood all the way up to controlling their access to a phone, car, and money in high school.

As I said in Chapter 1, the main problem with authoritarian and permissive parenting styles—including gentle parenting when it is permissive—is that they encourage self-preservation over the goal of connection. Thus, they may produce behavior that looks compliant and respectful to a point but is actually selfish and guarded. If we want to teach our children to be respectful with a heart of honor, then we can only do that by teaching them over and over again what it is that they are valuing and protecting through respectful behavior.

FUN TO BE WITH

In our home, the first tool we used to teach our kids respectful behavior was the concept of "fun," which my parents originally learned from Love and Logic and used with me and my brothers growing up. When the yelling, tantrums, throwing things, or any other undesirable behavior appeared, we said, "That's no fun." If the child refused to stop the behavior, we offered them a choice: "Fun? Or room?" They then learned that they would stay in their room until they decided to be "fun to be with."

"Fun to be with" does not mean entertaining or silly. It means enjoyable, pleasant, and respectful. That is who we want to be and who we want to be around. It doesn't mean we can't have a bad day or be emotional. It means we don't hang out for very long with people who are out of control with their emotions or are taking them out through angry, mean, rude, or obnoxious behavior. If that is what you're going to do, then I'm going to put some space between us until you're respectful again. "Fun to be with" is the standard of respect and honor that is expected in our home.

The nice thing about introducing this standard in toddler land is that you are big and they are small. When you say, "Fun? Or room?" you have the power to pick them up and put them in their room if necessary. This lesson is much harder if you start when they're school-age or teenagers.

When Delani was a toddler first learning about "fun," here's how the interactions went down. Delani would start throwing a fit about something and I would set the boundary: "Are you going to be fun? Or do you need to go to your room?"

When she continued to flip out, I would ask, "Do you want to walk, or do you want me to carry you to your room?"

Sometimes she went, and sometimes carrying was necessary. A minute later, she would reappear.

"Are you ready to be fun?" (Scream of rage.) "Okay, you're not ready to be fun. Do you want to walk or want me to carry you?"

Then she would run back to her room because she didn't want me to touch her, and I would hear her screaming from her room with the door open. So I would walk in and say, "Hey, that's fine. Do you want to be quiet or do you want me to close the door?"

When she continued to scream, I would say, "Okay, no problem," and then leave the room and close the door.

The first time I did this, she immediately ran to the door to open it again, so I said, "Hey, you can be quiet and have the door open, or Mommy is going to keep the door closed." I then closed the door on my screaming, enraged child and held the doorknob closed so she couldn't open it.

After playing this scene a couple more times, I was done with the doorknob holding, so I asked Ben to switch the knobs around so we could lock the room from the outside. The first time we locked the door, she kicked and beat the door like mad. But Ben said, "As soon as you're calm and quiet, I will open the door." (Don't worry, we never locked the door and walked away—we always stood there waiting for her. We just didn't want to add smashed fingers to the party, and thankfully we only had to lock the door a few times before she stopped screaming altogether.)

The moment she was quiet, we opened the door. "Are you ready to be fun and clean up your mess?" I would ask brightly. If she was still grouchy faced, I would offer, "I will keep the door open as long as you are respectful." But if she said, "Fun," with a smile, I would say, "Awesome!" And that would be it . . . until the next round.

This is the hardest part. "Fun or room" is not a one and done lesson. Everyone's hoping for the superglue effect, but that only works with the simplest tasks and behaviors. When you're building values, habits, character, and a culture, those only come through *lots* of repetition. You are training your child to understand how the concept of "fun" and "not fun" applies in many scenarios. They also need to *practice* being fun. (And let's be honest—many of us adults still need more practice being fun.) To this day, when things are getting a bit wild, disrespectful, or we can sense that the standard for honor in our family is not being upheld, Ben or I simply say to our now teenage daughters and nearly middle-school-aged son, "Do you guys want to be fun or take it somewhere else?"

HASSLE TIME

As our kids got a bit older, we started to implement another tool my dad picked up from Love and Logic: "hassle time." Hassle time is a great way to teach kids that when they are creating an environment of chaos or conflict, it is disrespectful and dishonoring to the other people who are unwilling victims of this experience.

Here's how it works. Say that you are taking a family road trip to Disneyland from Northern California (yes, I have firsthand experience with this) and you hit the Grapevine—the last winding, traffic-ridden forty miles of Interstate 5 before you reach Los Angeles. Your kids, understandably restless after seven hours in the car, decide that this is the perfect time to start antagonizing each other with hitting, yelling, crying, and tossing any objects in reach. Now, your instinctive response would be to see how far your arm can reach behind you from the front seat to slap something and hope you can convince them you mean it when you say, "You do not want me to stop this car right now!" But instead of jumping in and escalating the chaos, you simply say, "Hey, guys, just so you know—I'm feeling hassled. And I'm starting the clock right now."

Now the first time you do this, your children won't know what you're talking about and they'll most likely continue with the bickering and crying. That's okay. You just let the clock run, and then when they finally calm down, you let them know, "Okay, it took you thirty minutes to stop being disrespectful. The current exchange rate in this family is that thirty minutes of hassle time equal one hour of time that each of you owe me. I will let you know when I want to use those hours."

So you go and have a great time at Disneyland together and then you come home. Then one of your kids reminds you that their best friend's birthday party is coming up on Saturday—something they really want to do. This gives you a great point of leverage. So you say, "Hey, do you remember when we were driving to Disneyland and you kept hitting your brother and started the war that happened in the car? You racked up an hour of hassle time with that one. So I would love to take you to your friend's birthday party on Saturday as soon as you have worked off your hassle time. It's Thursday afternoon. So you've got from now until three o'clock on Saturday to get your hassle time done. You can even pick how you work it off. Do you want to wash the cars? Rake all the leaves in the backyard? Clean the bathrooms in the house? You pick."

"I don't want to do any of those."

"I know. Do you want to decide or do you want me to decide?"

"I'll rake the leaves."

"Okay, great. So just to confirm, you're going to rake the leaves for your hassle time and you're going to have this done before three o'clock on Saturday."

"Yeah, cool."

"And you know where to find the rakes and gloves and bags for the leaves?"

"Yes."

"And you know what I want a raked yard to look like, right? We've done it before."

"Yes."

"Okay, come find me and tell me when it's done."

So as with any lesson you are teaching your child, it's essential that you are prepared to follow through and do what you say, no matter what they do. You have done your job and clarified and confirmed that they understand what is expected of them. Now it's on them to make a choice and experience the consequences. Try not to micromanage them as they work this out. On Saturday morning, maybe you give them a nudge. "Hey, I just wanted to give you a helpful reminder. I see the backyard is still covered with leaves. It's ten in the morning now. The birthday party is fifteen minutes from our house, so you might want to be ready to go by 2:45. That gives you about four hours to get that hassle time worked off. Are you good?"

"Yeah."

Now I don't know about your children, but if they're like mine, there's a high chance that they do not manage their time and get their chore done. The next thing you know, it's 2:30 p.m. and they're running to you saying, "Hey, Mom, I'm ready to go."

"Oh, are the leaves done?"

"No."

"Okay, well, I would love to take you to the party when the leaves are done."

"Can't I do it when I get back?"

"I know you'd love that. But I would love to take you to the party as soon as the leaves are done."

"Are you serious?"

"I am serious."

"What?!"

And this is where you may be met with some pushback and more disrespectful behavior. Keep calm and keep smiling, because this is a truly wonderful and remarkable moment of treasured learning that your precious child is experiencing in front of you. If he runs to the backyard and rakes the leaves in time for you to take him to the party, great. If he takes his time because he's sulking and trying to get away with a job half done, so you have to keep sending him back to finish and he ends up missing the party, then it's extra sad for him, but it also means this lesson is going to be even more memorable. There is nothing but winning for you in this lesson—as long as you are managing your own respect levels and continuing to show empathy and protect connection in the process.

So often we shortcut introducing consequences for disrespect or any undesirable behavior because we are uncomfortable allowing our child to experience failure. But remember, failure is a powerful and essential piece of the learning process. Instead of protecting them from failure, what we want and need is to help guide them through low-cost failure that will teach them what they need to learn to avoid high-cost failures. Also, it's in the midst of letting them experience the consequences of poor choices that our empathy can be especially effective and clear. We can let them rage and spew their "I hate yous" and come back with "I'm sincerely sorry you had to miss the party. It's such a bummer. I know you're upset. Don't worry, we can still take him his gifts at church. Thanks for getting the leaves done. The yard looks great. Next time I hope you can get them done before you have something you want to do. Now, I'm going to go ahead and go inside because I don't have any conversations with people who talk to me this disrespectfully. I love you." In everything we're sending the message "This is your choice and I am with you in the pain of the consequences, but I am not going to take them away."

Of course, they're probably not going to be happy about that and it may take them a while to think about what's happened. So maybe you give them till the next morning to see if they're ready to talk. "So why do you think this happened, buddy?"

"You wouldn't let me go to the party."

"That would be sad if that was the whole story. Let me know when you want to talk about it." As soon as I knew my child was truly ready to talk about the problem, I would remind them of where it all started. "Remember what happened back in the car on the way to Disneyland? You made a few choices in this process that got us to where we are today. I'm not okay with you disrespecting your brother like you did in the car. And I'm not okay with you taking your frustration and anger out on me like you did yesterday because you tried to dodge the consequences of that choice and encountered another consequence that was not fun for you. Is there anything you could have done differently?"

It's important to keep checking the temperature until they're ready to own the problem, face the pain and sadness that their choices have brought into their lives, and find a solution to the problem. Until then, any of your great advice is going to be casting pearls before swine. So be patient and trust your child to figure out what you are teaching them. Because when we don't get in the way of our own lessons, our kids truly are geniuses at learning them. If you're willing to walk through a missed birthday or similar tough consequence with them, then the next time you say, "I'm feeling hassled," they're probably going to adjust pretty quickly.

WATCHING FOR DIPS

As with all of these pillars we're trying to establish in our home, honor is not something we're going to be perfect at all the time. The unfortunate reality is that sometimes the disrespectful behavior we're reacting to is actually something our kids learned from us. This is not always the case, of course—I know for a fact that Lincoln did not learn to use knives to take out his frustration from us, because neither Ben nor I have ever destroyed property in anger. But those sarcastic retorts or critical comments we hear pop up from time to time? Sure they could have learned them from some movie or other kids on the playground. But they could also have picked them up from us. Yes, sometimes they could be ignoring the request to put away their Nintendo Switch at the dinner table because they are just stubborn and addicted to their entertainment. Or they could have observed that from time to time when we're on our phones, that's more important than being present with them. Kids naturally intuit that if we are doing it, then it must be okay. Unless we stop and clean up our disrespect, we are just greenlighting our kids to punch away on that big red button.

What we have learned to watch out for are not the major displays of disrespect, but the subtle things that cause the respect levels to dip just a little. The pillar of honor is held up by us consistently displaying high levels of value for each other and our relationships. This requires us to value things that matter to our spouse and kids that may not matter so much to us, so we must be vigilant that we don't neglect or devalue what's important to them. For example, when my kids were in preschool and early elementary, they became obsessed with *tiny toys*. Shopkins. Littlest Pet Shops. Legos. They spent hours each day playing with these things, and they wanted me to join in their fun. This was important to them, and my engagement with them in doing something they loved and cared about sent the message that I valued what mattered to them—even though personally I couldn't have cared less about tiny toys—and therefore valued them.

On other occasions, I'm sorry to say, I've sent the message that my value for what's important to them is low. At one point, Adalyn started asking me to help her pick out outfits for school and youth group. After a few incidents in which she rejected all of my suggestions, I started to get frustrated. The next time she asked me to help her, I asked with a hint of sarcasm,

"Okay, but are you going to wear any of the outfits I pick out?" We began the process of putting together outfits, but now in our comments back and forth, we were edging toward the sarcastic and critical. After she had rejected my suggestions yet again, I threw out, "Well, then, you can go naked." When I later confronted her about her disrespect, I started by apologizing for how I had joined the party and been disrespectful toward her too.

Part of showing value for what's important to our spouse and kids is understanding that they have different needs based on our different personalities (tools like DISC and the love languages are so helpful for helping identify and understand these needs!). These differences are going to affect what kind of experiences feel disrespectful or dishonoring to them. For example, I have a higher need for order, cleanliness, and peace than Ben does. So chaos, loud noises, and messiness feel disrespectful to me, where they don't as much for Ben. So the dance in our marriage is finding where we meet in the middle. How do we honor one another's needs without lowering our standards and expectations for what feels honoring and respectful to us? Basically I have learned to let things be a little messier a little longer, and Ben cleans things up and restores order a little sooner.

Another area where we have learned to be vigilant about dips in the level of value, respect, and honor we're displaying is in the way we communicate with each other—our words, our tone, our body language, and our engagement. Disrespectful communication doesn't have to include yelling, cursing, name-calling, or arguing. It simply demonstrates that we don't value the other person's thoughts, feelings, and needs in the way they deserve. Sometimes it looks like tuning people out or not taking them seriously. I have spent time around some families who use a lot of playfulness, joking, and sarcasm in their style of communication. Often it's perfectly fine, but it can also cross the line and become disrespectful. One family in particular has grown children now, and whenever I'm around them I'm struck by the way the adult son interacts with his mom. She will be in the middle of a conversation with someone, and he will interrupt her with sarcastic or mocking comments and physically invade her space with pokes and prods. Yet instead of confronting it or setting a boundary, she tolerates his behavior and allows it to intrude on her conversation because that's the culture in their home—disrespect cloaked in playfulness.

It's our job as parents to clarify, model, and protect the high standard of respect we want to require in our communication. This is something Ben and I worked hard on with our kids, though of course we have needed to be confronted ourselves at times when a family member feels the line of respect and honor has been crossed. Once, we were all going somewhere in the car, and apparently we were talking over one another more than I realized, and Delani finally piped up and said, "I have been trying to communicate with all of you all day. None of you are being very respectful." The timing and tone of her comment were humorous, so we all started laughing. But then I apologized and we all adjusted and reengaged the conversation with a lot more listening going on. It was beautiful to see Delani jumping in and holding us all up to the standard of respect in our family. This is the goal—to see our kids protecting the pillars we are building together.

GRATITUDE—THE HONOR BOOSTER

During a recent visit, my brother Taylor took Adalyn and Lincoln to the gas station to get snacks for a movie marathon they had spontaneously planned together. When they got back to the house, the kids ran to their rooms to get in pj's, and Taylor pulled me aside.

"Your kids are the most thankful kids I've ever been around," he said. "They each thanked me about five times while we were getting snacks. And it's not just when they're getting a treat. They say thank you whenever I do anything for them, and they always ask me if I need help with anything. It's such a contrast with my friends' kids or nieces and nephews. Practically every kid I meet just takes everything for granted. I constantly tell my friends about what my nieces and nephew are like."

Well, that warmed my mother's heart right up. It's one thing to see your kids behaving in front of you—it's another to hear that they're doing it when you're not around. And the behavior of gratitude is one that Ben and I have both been very intentional about practicing with our kids, because it is yet another—and maybe one of the most important—ways we try to cultivate the pillar of honor in our family.

Gratitude is showing value and appreciation for things, which means it is an expression of honor. Most importantly, the practice of gratitude trains us to *see* that value. The more we practice gratitude, the more grateful we feel, because we start seeing the world through a lens of appreciation. People who do not practice gratitude ignore the value in things around them, even though it's usually not hard to see.

I once had a client come to me and ask, "How do you teach your kids to be grateful? My child never says please or thank you. She just takes everything for granted."

"Well, how often do you say please and thank you to her?" I asked.

This mom immediately started laughing. "My husband would think it's so funny that that's the first thing you asked me," she said. "He's always telling me that I don't say please and thank you very much."

I shrugged. "How can you expect your child to practice a behavior that you're not modeling for her? It's not that she's incapable of gratitude. It's that you need to help her cultivate it."

In our family, Ben and I particularly try to show gratitude for the small, everyday things that each of our family members contributes to our home. In so many families, it's taken for granted when mom cooks a meal or does the dishes, when dad mows the lawn or takes out the trash, or when the kids clean their rooms or help with the laundry. But Ben and I try to say thank you to each other and to our kids for all of these contributions, which we genuinely appreciate. So every single time I see it, I thank my girls for doing the dishes or thank Lincoln for feeding the dog. We want our children to see their responsibilities not as onerous duties or obligations but as opportunities to willingly show value for the family members who directly value and benefit them. We want them to see all the ways their parents and siblings value them, because that helps to remind and enforce the high standard of respect we want and expect as we interact. And guess what? Whatever we show them is what they eventually show to us.

So this is the pillar of honor—maintaining high levels of value, respect, and appreciation for others through the way we speak and interact. We do this by:

- Demonstrating respect and appreciation through our words and actions
- Setting boundaries and introducing consequences for disrespectful behavior while maintaining our own level of respect (tools like "fun or room" and "hassle time" are both useful here)
- Walking through the consequences of disrespect with our kids so they can learn from them
- Cleaning up our messes when we are disrespectful
- Paying attention to "dips" in respect when thoughts, feelings, and needs are not valued or when words and communication become too sarcastic or critical
- Practicing gratitude

I think most people want to raise children who are honorable—that is, children who have values, standards, and integrity. But what we must understand is that we are helping them cultivate those values and standards every day by the value we express and the standard of respect we demonstrate and require in our home. It's in our family that they will learn to see others with eyes of honor, based on the way we see them.

6

The Structure of Connection: Self-Control and Responsibility

MANY YEARS AGO, WHEN I worked in the children's department at Bethel, I was assigned for a time to the preschool classroom on Sunday mornings. In most churches, the preschool class is glorified babysitting, but our team had a vision and goal of creating an environment where these four- and five-year-olds could learn about God and encounter the Holy Spirit. As I soon discovered, however, our team didn't really have a solid strategy for confronting threats to that environment—namely, out-of-control children.

There was one four-year-old boy, Liam, who was particularly rowdy and physical. The first day I was in the class with him, he got upset and chucked one of the kid-sized plastic chairs across the room. I quickly discerned that all the other children, and even the adult volunteers, who gave a gentle correction following the chair-throwing but did nothing to set a boundary with this behavior, were walking on eggshells around Liam trying not to upset him. Obviously this was not going to work with the culture we said we were hoping to create. So the next time he picked up something to throw, I grabbed it from him and said, "Oh buddy, wow, that is no fun. Do you want to be fun and respectful or are you all done in my classroom?"

Liam looked at me in fury, growled, and then swept his arm across the desk near him and knocked a cup of water and a pile of goldfish crackers onto the ground.

"Okay, no problem," I said. Then I turned to the team leader and said, "Please call his parents."

Ten minutes later, Liam's dad appeared at the classroom door. I escorted Liam into the hallway and told his father, "I'm sorry, but he can't be in the class."

Then I addressed Liam. "Buddy, I love when you're in our classroom and you choose to be happy and fun to be with. But you getting mad and destroying my classroom isn't working. I need a plan from you for how you're going to be safe and fun to be with in my class. You're welcome to come back as soon as you're able to do that."

Then I turned back to his dad and repeated the instruction. "I need a plan from him for how he's going to manage himself. Because he's out of control. I'm happy to have him as long as he can control himself."

Liam didn't come back to class for three weeks because I wouldn't let him in without a plan. Finally, he came holding this little piece of paper, which he could barely read. We sat down next to each other and I asked, "How are you going to do a good job so that angry, mad person doesn't come out? I'm okay if you're sad or you're frustrated. But that angry, mad person? He can't come to my classroom because it's scary."

"When I get mad, I just want to be alone," Liam said. "So I need a space to go and count."

"Okay, so how can I help you?" I asked. "I don't know when you're mad, but you do. So you need to be able to tell me when you're mad."

"I want to go to the bathroom to count. I'll tell you when I need to go."

So we tried out this plan. Sure enough, whenever Liam started to get angry, he began going to the bathroom so he could count and calm down. If the bathroom was occupied, we found a corner where he could stand, and it was my job to keep the other kids out of his space until he was ready to come back. And it worked. This four-year-old boy learned self-control in our classroom because that's what we required of him (even though it seemed the same expectation was not enforced at home). And he continued to use the same self-management techniques as he moved on into elementary school.

CONTROL VS. FREEDOM

The pillars of love and honor cannot stand strong without the pillar of self-control. Without self-control, there can be no connection between two people, because out-of-control people are not *safe*. Without self-control, there can be no honor, because honor depends upon the core conviction that human beings can and should not be controlled but can and must control themselves. As my dad loves to say, "You cannot control other people. The only person you can control—on a good day—is yourself." Love and honor are both free choices, and freedom—contrary to what many people think these days—does not mean the license to do whatever you want but the power to do what is loving, right, and good. If we want to be free, powerful people who choose and build loving, safe connections, then we must develop the pillar of self-control.

As parents, one of the most seductive lies we fall into believing is that it's actually our job to control our kids. It's really easy to do. When they come into the world, they're completely dependent on us to do everything for them. As they start growing up and we see just how much trouble and mess they can get into, it's tempting to think we should use tools of control and intimidation, because they do "work" to elicit compliant behavior—in some kids—in the short term. And then as they become teenagers and prepare to leave the nest, we naturally want to continue to support them and protect them from bad influences and decisions, and influence them toward good decisions.

But as we do these things, there is a delicate and sacred line between us and our children that we must learn to protect, and teach them to protect— at least if our goal is connection, not perfection. That line is that in a safe, loving, honoring relationship, control is *shared,* because each of us is controlling ourselves and our contribution to the relationship. When control is shared in a relationship, it becomes a safe place for both people to influence one another. And influence is what we want with our kids, not control. Influence in a relationship means I have access to your heart because you've given me that access. I didn't take it or coerce it out of you. You entrusted it to me. Shared control is the holy grail if we want to raise kids who will successfully launch into adulthood and independence and still hold on to their connection with us and remain open to our input.

Without the safety of shared control, our kids are naturally going to put up resistance or hide from us because they don't want to expose themselves to being controlled. Remember the "big red button"? Often, what is motivating our child's behavior in those situations is that they are experimenting with ways to control their environment to get what they want. And when we react to their attempts to get control by being out of control (this includes being passive/permissive toward their behavior) or controlling (aggressive/authoritarian) ourselves, it only sends the message that in relationships it's okay to not control ourselves and okay to try to control other people. This is not what we want, because again, both out-of-control and controlling behaviors are toxic to safe, loving, honoring connections. Engaged, connection-focused parenting looks like controlling ourselves and teaching our kids to control themselves.

I once had a client who was struggling in her relationships with her twenty-year-old daughter in college and a sixteen-year-old son still living at home. Her son was a talented basketball player who was already competing at the highest level in his state. He was also completely disrespectful toward his mom, flew into destructive fits of rage, and was abusing alcohol, drugs, and porn. Meanwhile, she told me she knew her daughter was sleeping with her boyfriend at college. Both relationships were almost completely disconnected, and this mom said her primary goal was restoring her connection.

As we investigated the causes for the disconnection, I asked this woman how she knew her daughter was sleeping with her boyfriend. She explained that she required both her kids to keep their location tracking active on their cell phones at all times, and that she constantly monitored where they were. She could see when her daughter was not in her dorm room. When I asked her why she required this of her kids, she said, "Well, I want to know where they are and what they're doing."

"And what are you going to do about it?" I asked.

"Well, I just know that if my son is at his friend's house, he is probably partying. Or if it shows that my daughter is at her boyfriend's all night that she's sleeping with him."

"Then what's going to happen?"

"Well, then I am just prepared that they might be drinking and having sex."

"And then what happens?"

"Well, then I just know."

"So your kids know that you're stalking where they are at all times. What is the goal here?"

"Well, it's just so that they can see that I know what they're doing. It's like extra accountability. It's why we took our son's door off his room when we found out he was doing porn."

"So what's the accountability after you find out they're doing these things?"

"Well, I mean, unless something happens, then nothing, really."

"What are you going to do if you know they're up to something you don't like?"

"Go find them and talk to them about it."

"So how is freedom and trust going to grow in these relationships? Because right now it just looks like you're trying to control them by letting them know you're watching them at all times, while also not enforcing any consequences for out-of-control and disrespectful behavior. It's passive-aggressive and sends the message that neither of you is going to control yourselves or require control from the other person. As long as this goes on, you're cutting off the possibility of connection and influence with your kids."

I ended up spending a year working with this mom, and gradually she gained awareness that many of the things she was doing with her kids were driven by fear. At one point I asked her, "What are you most afraid of?"

She said, "I'm afraid I'm going to lose one of my kids."

"Do you have any control over that?"

After a long pause, she finally said, "No, I guess not."

"So you're exhausting yourself trying to keep something from happening that you have no control over."

"Yeah."

Sadly, however, no matter how many times she told me she saw the problem and wanted to change, the next time we met she would confess that she had still been employing the same control tools. She just couldn't give them up—even when she could see that her fear of losing her kids was driving her to do things that would actually increase the likelihood of that happening. After a year, we stopped meeting.

Believe me, I have a lot of sympathy for this scared mom, and for all parents who are trying to figure out how to prepare their kids to manage their freedom in a world of options, many of which are terribly dangerous. Even when you start teaching your kids to control themselves from the time they're toddlers, and to share control in your relationship with them, there is so much vulnerability in the fact that we are responsible for these are little humans, who will face difficult choices, make mistakes, and struggle mightily as they grow up and go out into the world. This journey is not for the faint of heart. In fact, I'm convinced it's only possible to succeed by following the Holy Spirit and receiving massive amounts of His grace.

After all, He knows all about taking on the challenge of teaching kids to manage their freedom through love and connection instead of through fear and control. This is the story we're in—the story that began in the Garden where God gave humans freedom in a world with dangerous choices, that built to the incredible crescendo of Him sending His Son to deal with the consequences of our poor choice, and that continues with us now learning to walk in the Spirit of love, power, and self-control. Our ability to grow in self-control ourselves, and then to teach our kids to walk in self-control, flows from Him.

The more we plug into the Spirit of self-control, the better we will get at using tools of self-control. There are many tools we might explore, but here I will introduce you to the two tools that Ben and I have learned to use specifically when our kids start to throw out disrespectful or out-of-control behavior: one-liners and "fun" timeouts.

ONE-LINERS

The one-liners are another tool from Love and Logic, so once again, major kudos to them. They are:
"I know."
"Probably so."
"That could be."
"I don't know."
"Nice try."
These one-liners help you disable the big red button and resist allowing your child's out-of-control behavior to control your reaction. If you master these, you never have to argue with your child again. You can let them make a big, out-of-control mess without jumping in and adding your mess to it. Then, on the other side of the mess, you can focus on helping them clean theirs up instead of having to clean up yours at the same time.

When Delani was in sixth grade, she came to me one day after school and said she needed me to help her with some math homework due the following day.

"Well, I have time now or right after dinner," I told her. "But I told your brother and sister I would watch a show with them after that, so I can't do it before bedtime. You let me know what you want to do."

Of course, Delani got busy with everything but her homework, and the evening ticked by. Only when I was snuggling with Adalyn and Lincoln on the couch watching their show did she run up to me and say frantically, "Mom, we have to do my math. I can't let this be late. It's really important."

I had known this might be coming, so I was prepared. I needed my daughter to understand that her mismanagement of her responsibilities didn't automatically affect my plan for how I was managing my time for the evening. "Oh honey, I am so sorry, but I am hanging out with your brother and sister right now."

Delani's mouth fell in shock. "Are you kidding me? I'm going to get a bad grade on this."

"I'm really sorry," I said, sincerely but calmly. "I told you when I was available, and unfortunately, I'm no longer available right now."

"Oh my gosh! Do you want me to fail?"

"I don't know."

"You are the worst mom ever."

"That could be."

"Well, I'm glad you know you're the worst mom because I cannot believe you."

"Nice try."

Eventually, Delani stormed off, yelling all the way up the stairs and slamming the door.

After the show was over, I put Adalyn and Lincoln to bed, then opened the door to Delani's room and said, "Hey, I know we didn't get to your project, but if you'd like to try to find me in the morning, I'd love to help you as soon as this mess is cleaned up. I love you, sweet girl."

Delani ignored me, so I shut her door and went to bed. At six o'clock the next morning, I awoke to see two little brown eyes next to my bed staring at me.

"Mom."

"Yes, hi. What's going on?"

"I'm sorry about yesterday. I wasn't very nice. Can I have your help?"

"Sure. I'd love to help you. And you're right. Yesterday was not much fun. Let me get dressed."

I didn't lecture her or demand more apology in the moment. We got to work on her project, and I waited till she got home from school that day to pull her aside and ask, "So what could have happened differently last night?"

"Well, I should have asked for your help right then and not waited. Because then I got scared I would get a bad grade and was mad at you."

"Smart," I agreed. "So what do you think you'll do next time?"

"Oh I'll be getting your help right away when you have time!"

"Brilliant."

A big win for me was that I hadn't interrupted Delani learning this lesson by reacting with disrespect of my own. Using the one-liners is an extremely effective way of sending the message "Your disrespect or out-of-control won't control me. I manage myself. What are you going to do with you?" Controlling myself protected her in her learning process about the consequences of not managing herself.

TAKE A "FUN" BREAK

Another effective tool for self-control is taking a break if you realize you are on the verge of being "not fun" because you've reached an unhealthy level of exhaustion, frustration, anger, and anxiety in the face of your kids' chaos and demands. I know that either sounds way too simple and obvious or might trigger a few eye rolls, because who has time for a break when their kids are driving them crazy? Well, I know it's not always possible to do, but there is science behind this. When stress reaches an intolerable level and our sense of well-being becomes threatened, our sympathetic nervous system gets triggered and automatically revs up a "fight or flight" reaction. If we don't interrupt this reaction, we basically go into autopilot. Our cognitive brain function goes down and our body and emotional brain basically take over. Unfortunately when this happens, we are essentially out of control. To regain control over our thoughts, emotions, and bodies, we need to find a way to get our bodies and brains out of stress and back into calm, and one of the best ways to do this, if you can, is by taking a break. This is exactly what four-year-old Liam figured out in my Sunday school class! It turns out that adults can use the same tool when they get stressed and overwhelmed.

My favorite memory of employing this tool happened one evening when Lincoln was five, Adalyn was seven, and Delani was twelve. We were making the ten-minute drive home after a church leadership meeting, and the kids were just crazy. I really don't know what got into them, because they were behaving in ways I had never really seen them behave. The moment we got in the car, the girls started fighting over something, and it soon escalated to slapping. I whipped around and told them I was starting the "hassle time" clock, but they continued to bicker, unfazed. Ben looked at me with an incredulous grin, clearly thinking the same thing—*What has gotten into them?*

Seconds later, I felt something hit me in the back of the head. I picked up the projectile and realized it was a chicken nugget. Lincoln's giggle from the backseat instantly betrayed the culprit. A few minutes later, another nugget flew past my ear. Turning around, I was flabbergasted to see a gallon-sized paper bag in Lincoln's lap and another chicken nugget clutched in his hand. I had no idea where this bag of nuggets had come from or how many were left inside, but Lincoln's gleeful face told me he was more than ready to keep chucking them all over the car. Meanwhile Ady and Lani were continuing to argue and now began asking Lincoln to share the nuggets with them.

It only took moments for me to register that I was heading into the danger zone. I could feel the changes in my body—a racing heartbeat, flushed face, and nostrils flaring with furious breathing. I was about to morph into Mom-Hulk. Thankfully, I spotted a gas station up ahead on the corner, and I knew, *We need to stop so I can take a break and stop the transformation.* So I turned to Ben and said, "We need gas."

"But we're fine," he said, glancing at the gauge.

"No, we need to stop," I insisted.

So Ben, probably discerning that the lives, or at least the backsides, of our kids were at stake in this moment, pulled into the gas station. I unbuckled my seatbelt, turned to the back of the car, made laser-like eye contact with each of my three children, and said firmly, "All of you stay in the car." I then looked meaningfully at Ben, indicating that he should join me in exiting the vehicle. Once outside, I could see three confused and upset faces staring out at us through the car window, but I could already feel the relief of no longer being trapped in the insane, chaotic atmosphere they'd been creating. Meanwhile Ben was looking at me with raised eyebrows that clearly asked, "So . . . what are we doing here?"

"Do you want to get some ice cream?" I asked.

"What?"

"Do you want ice cream?" I repeated.

He laughed and said, "Sure."

So I went into the gas station while Ben waited with the car full of crazy kids, bought two ice cream bars, came back out, and handed one to Ben. "You and I are the only ones in that car who were fun to be with," I explained. "So we get ice cream."

We then stood there beside the car, eating our ice cream slowly and with relish, and making sure the kids had a clear view of us the entire time. With each sweet bite, I could feel my composure and peace returning. When we were almost done, I opened the door to the backseat and calmly asked, "All right, are you guys ready to be fun? Or am I still running hassle time?" By this point, Lincoln was crying, his arms and legs stretched out in front of him begging to join us for ice cream. Adalyn was indignant and Delani furious, and both began throwing out excuses as to why they were not at fault and that it wasn't fair they didn't get ice cream too.

I endured about twenty seconds of this, then said, "Okay, it doesn't sound like anybody's ready to be fun," and shut the door. "Do you want another ice cream?" I asked Ben.

"No, I don't need another one," Ben laughed again.

"Okay, I don't either. Let's just hang out."

So we stood there by the car for another ten minutes or so, chatting about the evening and laughing together. At last I heard silence from the car, so I opened the door again and asked, "Are you guys ready to be fun and go home?" Three solemn faces nodded at me. So Ben and I got back in the car and resumed the journey, which remained blissfully quiet the entire time. When we arrived, I told the kids they would have hassle time the next day, and sent them to get ready for bed. They never behaved with that level of craziness on a car ride again.

The "fun" break tool doesn't have to be long to be effective. Ten to twenty minutes is usually enough, as long as you are actively using it to get yourself back to "fun," which means a calm state where you feel like you're back in control. Connecting with your spouse or a friend who is not freaking out can be really helpful, because you can co-regulate with their calm state. Prayer, meditation, or even a short walk can also restore self-control and positive emotions, like peace and joy.

One of the lessons we learn from the "fun" break tool is that self-care helps us regain self-control. We hear a lot about self-care these days, but too often it looks like indulgence or trying to create some stress-free bubble where we can escape the world. In the real world of marriage, parenting, and work, self-care is more often about physically, mentally, and emotionally recovering from a stress state and cultivating a calm state so we can reengage with our challenges and demands with self-control instead of a "fight or flight," passive or aggressive reaction. These reactions are always damaging to connection because they send the message "You are a threat, and I need to protect myself from you." Self-care that brings us back to calm supports the pillar of self-control by helping us respond well to crises and moments of chaos.

So that is the pillar of self-control, which we build by:

- Refusing to control or be controlled by others
- Giving our focus to controlling ourselves
- Using one-liners and other tools that help us maintain our self-control in the face of disrespect
- Taking "fun" breaks or practicing other types of self-care to move from a stress state to a calm state and regain control

THE ABILITY TO RESPOND

This brings us to the fourth of the Seven Pillars—the pillar of responsibility. As my dad often points out, the word "responsibility" means "response + ability"—the ability to respond. As the pillar of self-control teaches us, most things in life are not under our control, but what we do control is ourselves, and specifically, our responses. Our responses are where we exercise our power of free will to make choices.

The pillar of responsibility grows strong in our lives and relationships the more we learn to respond instead of react. The main difference between these two is the level of rational thought and choice involved. Reactions happen at a subconscious level—think of chemicals reacting in a test tube.

The word "response" comes from the root word "to answer." It implies that there is an intelligent process and an interpersonal exchange going on, a conversation with listening, critical thinking, and articulate messages being communicated. When we go into reaction mode, we end up floundering in the ocean of our emotions, looking for anything to grab on to for support. We're in survival mode looking for control, because we feel like our control is being threatened. When we're in response mode, we're securely in a boat with a rudder, pointing toward our goal. We may have to row hard against some waves and headwinds, but we maintain control of our vessel (us) and where we are steering it.

So what keeps us in the boat of responding and out of the ocean of reacting? Two things. The first is a core belief that we are responsible to manage us. This responsibility doesn't come from us or any other human—it comes from God. He is the One who gave us our lives to steward and our free will to make choices, and we are ultimately accountable to Him for what we do with that responsibility. One of the messages I am constantly sending my children is, "You are in charge of you all day. It's no one else's job to manage your life." From the time they were tiny, I would ask them, "Who is in charge of Delani? Who is in charge of Adalyn? Who is in charge of Lincoln?" I kept asking until they said, "I am." Of course, that doesn't mean they get to use their freedom however they want, and it's Ben's and my job to teach and enforce that the life they've been given to manage comes with duties and obligations, boundaries and rules, choices and consequences. We must honor the weight of their responsibilities like we honor our own responsibilities, which again, brings us back to the critical importance of leadership and modeling—we can only teach children to manage their freedom, make great choices, and learn from the consequences of poor choices to the degree that we have done and are doing that ourselves.

The second thing that keeps us in the responsibility boat is having a plan. I have a plan for what I'm going to do with me no matter what my husband or child chooses to do with them. Most parents know that their child is capable of being disrespectful or hurting another child or lying or throwing a tantrum—things all children have always done. But they don't necessarily know what they're going to do when it happens. Not having a plan guarantees that we're going to fall back into instinctive, fear-driven reactions that are not going to help our child learn to manage him or herself. Of course, having a plan doesn't mean you'll execute it perfectly—it's going to be a process of testing, refining, and lots of practice and repetition. Our kids are geniuses at exposing the flaws and weaknesses in our plan to stay calm and out of reaction mode as we teach and disciple them toward making good choices and becoming responsible. But if we stay engaged in the learning process with them, quickly clean up our messes, and take ownership for our choices, we will succeed in building and protecting the pillar of responsibility in our families.

CHOICES AND CONSEQUENCES

Guiding our children toward making good choices should begin, if possible, when they're little, and we do it by offering them good choices and then enforcing the consequences of their choices. Giving good choices is another tool I first learned about from Love and Logic, and as I soon discovered, it is a skill, even an art, that takes time and practice to hone. It's best to start small with things that don't really matter—"Do you want the red fork or the green fork?"—and then progress to things that matter a bit more—"Do you want one piece of broccoli or two?" It's also best to try to give choices all the time. This takes some intentionality, because we naturally default to what we would do or choose in a situation, and then just tell our kids to do that or make the choice for them. We have to interrupt that habit and form a new habit of constantly introducing our children to a world of choices. Yes, we are inserting our preferences in the choices we are giving them, and teaching them what we believe would be good and desirable for them. But we are protecting their opportunity to respond to that choice.

The first and most important rule of thumb in giving choices is that both options you offer will make you happy. Whether they eat one piece of broccoli or two, they're eating vegetables, which is what you want them to do. The second rule of thumb is that at some point, and maybe even quite often, your child *is* going to refuse either option or throw out other options, so that's where you need a plan to enforce boundaries and consequences.

Three other Love and Logic tools that work brilliantly in these situations are "Oh no! What are you going to do?" and "No problem."

"Oh no! What are you going to do?" is the tool to pull out whenever your child comes to you with a problem and tries to make it yours. Say your toddler drops their snack all over the floor. Instead of freaking out or rushing to clean it up for them, you say, "Oh no! What happened?"

"I dropped it!"

"What are you going to do?"

"Pick it up?"

"That's a great idea! You don't want the puppy to eat it!"

"No problem" is what you say to your kid when they try to refuse, ignore, or otherwise opt out of a choice you're giving them or a responsibility you're requiring them to take care of. It's a bit of a Jedi mind trick, because it actually means, "No problem for me, but there's a problem coming up for you if this is your choice." It is a signal that consequences are incoming for them.

One of my favorite stories about "No problem" is one my dad used to tell during parent training meetings. After copious begging and promises that he will be responsible to feed and care for it, a boy convinces his parents to get him a dog. However, within a few weeks he begins to slack on his duties. After a few days of giving her son multiple reminders to feed the dog and finally stepping in and doing the chore herself out of compassion for the starving dog, this boy's mother reaches her limit. One evening before dinner, she approaches him and said, "Buddy, I've ended up feeding the dog for you the last three nights but I'm not going to do that anymore. We agreed when we got the dog that feeding it was your job. So I need to know when you're going to feed the dog tonight because it's dinnertime. Would you like to do it right now or in five minutes?"

"In five minutes."

"Okay, great. So in five minutes, are you going to come tell me? Or should I just assume that the dog is fed."

"I'll feed it."

"Okay, so in five minutes, I'm going to assume that you went and fed the dog."

"Yeah."

"Because everyone in this household gets fed dinner one time, right?"

"Sure."

Well, five minutes later the mom checks on the dog's bowl and it's dry and empty. The dog has not been fed. So she goes and finds her son, who's playing a video game, and says, "Hey, buddy, it looks like you didn't feed the dog."

"I'm gonna do it in a minute."

"Okay, no problem."

Fifteen minutes later, the mom announces that dinner is ready. Her son arrives at the dinner table to find that everyone has a plate of food except for him.

"Mom, where's my food?" he asks.

"Well, you didn't feed the dog and that's your job. Everyone gets fed one time, so I gave your plate to the dog. Feel free to sit with us while we eat dinner, or if you'd like to be excused to get started on your homework, you can do that."

Upset and shocked, the boy leaves the table and spends the rest of the evening working on his homework.

The next evening, his mom asks, "Hey, are you going to feed the dog now or in five minutes?"

"I can feed him now, Mom!" he says, immediately jumping up. Seconds later, she hears the sound of kibbles hitting the dog's bowl. "I fed him, Mom!" he calls.

"Thanks, honey."

Of course, the only way "No problem" works is if you are willing to give your child's food to the dog. You know they're not going to be happy with this consequence and will likely make that known. But one evening dealing with their frustration and discomfort, followed by them making a real adjustment in their behavior, is far more effective and relatively painless compared to what we usually try first, which is to take the consequence of their irresponsibility on ourselves and then complain and lecture our child about what's not okay. Many words without meaningful action is how our voices turn into the muted trombone voices in the Peanuts cartoon—"Womp womp womp." Meaningful action is what gives those two words—"No problem"—authority and weight.

MY HALF OF US

If we want connection to be the ultimate, overarching goal in our family, then our priority in modeling and teaching our kids responsibility is *not* just going to be focused around them cleaning their room, doing their homework, completing their chores, managing their allowance, or other individual responsibilities. Obviously we should require them to manage those, but we want to show them that all of these responsibilities are connected to something deeper, which is that each person in the family is responsible for their half of the relationship with every other family member. This means we reinforce that they're not just responsible to take care of their stuff and their jobs around the house; they're also responsible for how they are showing up in their attitude and behavior, and how these are affecting others.

When Adalyn turned twelve and entered sixth grade, she started going to youth group on Sunday evenings. We knew this was a big deal for her, but we had no idea how big it actually was. Adalyn has always been petite and behind her peers in physical development, and as she reached this last of her preteen years, she was absolutely desperate to fit in with her maturing adolescent friends. Week after week, "getting ready for youth group" became an ever longer, more elaborate, and more emotional process as Adalyn agonized over what to wear and how to do her hair and makeup. Eventually, this process spilled over into the rest of the week, to the point where she was planning outfits on Tuesday for youth group on Sunday. These planning sessions escalated into full Project Runway-like fashion shows, where we gave her input on multiple looks as she tried them on.

It didn't take long before none of us were having much fun with Adalyn going to youth group. From the time she was little, Adalyn has displayed a tendency to take her frustration, fear, and sadness out on others with sass, rude comments, and sarcasm. We had worked on this with her over the years, and she had improved in doing it less and cleaning up her messes more quickly. But with this new social experience dominating her life and apparently triggering some of her deepest insecurities and desires for belonging, verbal lashings-out from Adalyn became a weekly event.

After several weeks of this, I was ready to pull the plug on youth group altogether. I pulled Ben aside and said, "We need to have a conversation with Adalyn. She is caring more about how she looks and what her peers think of her at youth group than what youth group is supposed to be about. And I really am not a fan of what I'm seeing come out of her as a result."

"Yeah, I've been noticing that," he agreed.

"Okay, can we do this together? Because I'm so frustrated with her, I'm not sure I'll do a very good job by myself."

So one Sunday afternoon, before Adalyn began her preparation ritual, we pulled her aside and Ben took the lead. "Honey, we need to talk with you a little bit about how we're experiencing you getting ready for youth group. We totally understand that you want to wear an outfit that makes you feel good. But in the process what we're seeing is that our sweet, fun Ady is turning into this disrespectful person. We're not sure what is motivating this, but it seems like you're trying to change who you are to be accepted by someone else. We don't know if that's true, but we're hoping that's not what is driving your heart."

Ben then went on and explained to Ady how he saw her—that she was beautiful, valuable, and perfectly designed by God just the way she was. Clearly he was hitting the mark, because she began to cry. Ben and I both knew that the truths he was declaring over her were directly confronting some lies she'd been struggling with.

"We love you so much," I assured her. "We want to be there for you as you are stepping into this new adventure of middle school and youth group. No one's mad at you. No one's disappointed in you. But changing who you are and being disrespectful to everyone are scary for us. You're a powerful person and you have a powerful place in this family. And we know you want to take care of our hearts, so we need to let you know that this is not a fun experience and we need something different from you."

We hugged Ady as she continued to weep. After a few minutes, she gathered herself and asked us, "What do you need from me?" There was our daughter, speaking our family language and taking responsibility.

"We just need you to be aware of how you're impacting us. And we also need our Ady to not disappear."

Not only did Adalyn stop the disrespect, but after that conversation she began to open up to us about the fears she had been battling. Middle school had introduced her to levels of criticism and judgment she had never experienced before, and she had become terrified that she wouldn't fit in or be liked. In that place of trust and connection with her heart, we were able to speak to those fears, remind her of who she is, and call her to be courageously herself no matter what.

We have seen this time and time again—when we invite our kids to be responsible for our connection and not just their behavior, we are more likely to create the opportunity for them to discover what's going on in their heart that's driving their behavior. We become partners helping them grow in self-awareness of what is influencing the choices they're making and become more powerful in making responsible choices that protect connection as a result.

So that's the pillar of responsibility—cultivating the ability to respond, not react, by making good choices that are consistent with who we want to be. We do this, and help our kids do this, by:

- Understanding that it's our job to manage our responses to whatever happens
- Having a plan for how we will respond to our child's disrespectful or out-of-control behavior
- Offering our child choices and enforcing the consequences of their choices
- Helping our child understand that they are not just responsible for their behavior and choices, but they are also responsible for their half of relationship with us

7

The Structure of Connection: Trust and Faith

I ONCE HAD A NEWLY divorced mother come to me for coaching on what to do about her relationship with her seventeen-year-old daughter. This girl had begun to act out dramatically in the wake of her parents' divorce—sneaking out of the house, drinking, doing drugs, and sleeping with her boyfriend. The mother had tried everything she knew to rein in her daughter, but their relationship had only deteriorated further. Then one evening they had gotten into an argument, which escalated to the point where the daughter threatened to kill herself and her mother, and then threw a knife at her mom. The mother had called the police, who came and put her daughter in a 5150 hold until they decided she wasn't a danger to herself or others. After the girl was released, the mother had taken her to a number of psychiatrists, who had diagnosed her as bipolar and put her on medication. This had seemed to help the girl calm down, but her mother knew the pills were only helping symptoms, not root causes.

"So what is our goal in working together?" I asked this woman at our first session, after hearing her saga. "What does a win in this situation look like?'

"I just want to restore my relationship with my daughter," the mom said immediately. "The problem is that I can't trust her. I can't trust her with a phone, a job, a car . . . right now she doesn't even have a bedroom door or furniture, except a mattress, because she's been so volatile."

"That's a tough one," I agreed. "Can I ask, do you know your daughter's primary love languages?"

She didn't know them, so finding that out was the first homework assignment I gave her. I explained that there were two messages she needed to start sending to her daughter. The first was "I love you, and my goal is connecting with you heart to heart." This was where intentionally speaking her love languages would come in. The second message was "My goal is not to control you but to empower you." The best way to communicate this, I told her, was by offering choices, and reassured her this didn't mean letting the girl do whatever she wanted. Since her daughter was so out of control, I encouraged this mom to start really small, almost at an elementary level, with the choices she offered her. Did she want chicken or burgers for dinner? Did she want to go to the store with her mom or stay home?

I met with this client twice a month for six months. At each session, she reported to me what she had done to speak her daughter's love languages, which choices she had been offering, and how her daughter was responding. It actually didn't take very long for the daughter to show that she was starting to feel trusted and valued by her mom. They began having some honest conversations about their relationship and the daughter even felt free to give her mom some feedback about the painful things that had unfolded with the divorce. Eventually they broached the tougher questions of whether the daughter was ready to have furniture back in her room, or could handle the freedom and responsibility of access to a phone and car.

After six months, the mom was so pleased with the progress she had made with her daughter that we agreed to stop having sessions unless something came up and she needed my help. I didn't hear from her for months, and then she called me asking if she could see me to discuss some work challenges she was facing. At the end of the call, I asked, "How's your daughter doing?"

"Oh, it's going so well!" she exclaimed warmly. "Our relationship feels so good. We have lots of trust and value, respect and love. She has a job and got her phone back. And we're having fun together. We just celebrated her eighteenth birthday and we both went and got our noses pierced!"

After we hung up, I marveled at the turnaround in a parenting relationship that had been so broken the child had thrown a knife at her mom, to now being so restored that they were getting their noses pierced together. I had to give this mom the credit. She really got in there and did the heavy lifting of being fully engaged in pursuing connection with her daughter. She didn't cower in the face of her crazy behavior or react with control. She set the boundaries and then daily put in countless reps offering love and trust to her daughter in small, incremental ways. She was consistent in sending the messages of love and shared control, and it was this consistency that made her daughter believe she was sincere. And because her daughter responded well to the offer to return her mother's trust and love and be empowered to control herself, her freedom, and her responsibilities, together they built a brand-new relationship, better than they'd ever had.

TRUST AND "TRUTHING"

The pillar of trust is one many of us might list first if we were asked, "What is the most important element in a relationship?" Even more than love or respect, what we really need to open our hearts to a long-term connection with another human being is trust. But what is trust, and how do we cultivate it?

The Oxford American Dictionary defines "trust" as "firm belief in the reliability, truth, ability, or strength of someone or something." Trust grows the more we convince one another that our goal in the relationship truly is a loving, safe, respectful, responsible connection. We do this through consistently engaging in what my dad refers to as "the exchange of truth" or "truthing." Every day, everything we do communicates whether we are living authentically in the truth of who we say we are and want to be, or whether there are gaps of inconsistency in the truth we're living.

Wherever we are living out gaps in the truth, we will inevitably send mixed messages to those around us, which will erode our ability to reach the goal of building secure trust. If that mother had been speaking her daughter's love languages one minute and then trying to control her the next, she would not have created the opportunity for real trust to grow. Unfortunately, it's all too easy to send mixed messages. Here are a couple examples I've seen come up often in parenting. First, there's the "count to five" technique. It's one thing to give your child a time limit when enforcing choices—"Are you going to feed the dog now or in five minutes?" But so often what I've observed is parents using the "count to five" to procrastinate in getting fully engaged in a situation. They often don't really have a plan for what they're going to do when they get to five, and they are essentially telling their child that between one and four, they're allowed to mess with them. If they do have a plan, it often looks like punishment. So the first mixed message this sends is, "I'm parenting you, but please don't make me get involved. Please let me stay disengaged in this situation." The second is, "Even though I say my goal is a safe, loving connection and shared control, I will also try to control you with the threat of punishment."

There is another version of "count to five" that I have witnessed many times now, and it looks like "100 questions and suggestions."

"Did the dog get fed today? No? Oh, I bet he's hungry. Do you think you could contribute and do this chore? I know it's not your favorite. Do you want to tell me about what you *do* love doing? Maybe we can look at changing your chore to a different one that you like more. Would that feel better? I appreciate you telling me how this feels. What should we do about the dog getting fed? I understand you don't want to do it."

My first thought when I saw this approach was, "Who has time to have this exchange about everything you need to get your child to do?" If every request we make as a parent becomes a therapy session, the dog will never get fed! I do want to be connected to my child's heart and know their frustrations. But life will be full of situations that require them to do something they don't feel like doing, so teaching them that when they don't "feel" like it they can get out of a job is not a message that will set them up for success later on. Also, the longer we delay a consequence or boundary for them not doing what we're asking them to do, the more we are sending the message that it's okay for them not to do it.

Another mixed message parents often send when they're delivering discipline or consequences is saying something like, "I really don't want to spank you or keep you home from your friend's party or take away your phone, but I have to." Or they say, "What you did hurt my heart so much." In both cases, on the surface they are sending the message "I'm holding you accountable for your choices because that's my job as your parent," but doing it in a way that also suggests, "You're not just responsible for your behavior; you're also responsible for my actions and emotions." This is different from genuine empathy, which says, "I'm sad for you and the pain of the consequences you're going to experience for your choice." Parental empathy focuses on the child's experience, not their own. These mixed messages that subtly shift what is actually the parent's responsibility—their actions and emotions—onto the child can easily slip toward blame, shame, and emotional manipulation.

And perhaps the most obvious mixed message we can send is when we do something that falls below the standard of behavior we are requiring of them and act like it's okay. We speak disrespectfully and then tell them to be respectful. We tell them to be grateful but never say please or thank you ourselves. We tell them to do their chores but neglect our own responsibilities. This hypocrisy sends the message that there are two sets of rules in the house, one for the parents and one for the children. Our kids will naturally intuit that this double standard is not safe for trust and connection.

To close these gaps in the messages we're sending and practice truthing effectively, we need to accept two things. First, we must understand that it is more about what we do than what we say. It's what we do that convinces others that our words have weight. Especially when it comes to parenting our kids—and specifically enforcing choices, consequences, and boundaries—both my parents and Ben and I ascribe to a guiding principle: "Few words, meaningful actions." So many parents fall into the trap of using too many words when they're trying to require something from their kids and then not backing it up with actions. This is how you get word *inflation*. If you just keep printing word money without any gold standard of action to back it up, the value of your words will drop until they have basically become practically worthless. If you want to keep your word value high, make them more scarce and show just how meaningful they are by doing what you say.

The second thing we must understand about truthing is that we will only be successful in exchanging the truth with others to the degree that we are willing to exchange the truth with ourselves. In particular, the most important thing we must be honest about with ourselves is the goal we are actually pursuing in life and relational situations. Remember, in every human heart, the war of connection is constantly raging between our fear-driven instinct for self-preservation and our love-driven desire for love and connection. Until we are willing to look honestly in the mirror, most of us are not going to be fully aware of just how much fear and self-preservation are driving us, no matter how much we say connection is our goal. We can pick up the tools in this book and try to use them, but because our goal is actually something more like, "I want you to obey and comply because I want to stop feeling like a failure as a parent," or "Your mistakes and mess scare me," what is going to come out of us is not going to be honoring, loving, or empowering. We have to be able to face our insecurities, the lies we're believing, the unhealthy ways we're trying to meet our own needs, and the old habitual defaults to control, disrespect, and punishment if we hope to bring our internal world into alignment with the goal of connection and live out that truth.

Of course, there is massive grace for this process. We are called to model maturity for our children while we are also maturing ourselves, and we will make plenty of messes along the way. The key is that we don't just endlessly say "sorry" and then go back to doing what we were doing. We are cleaning up our messes every time by actively repenting—changing the way we think, speak, and behave—as we battle to know and live the truth more deeply.

TRUTHING ABOUT SEX

The real litmus test for whether we are truthing successfully and building the pillar of trust in our family is the degree to which each family member is open about the truths that make all of us feel most vulnerable—our thoughts, beliefs, values, feelings, needs, desires, hopes, dreams, fears, pain, and struggles. Such openness is evidence that we feel safe to entrust our family members with access to our hearts, and also that we have a courageous commitment to building and protecting our heart-to-heart connections with each other.

When it comes to truthing our kids, we certainly need wisdom to discern what they are ready to handle mentally, spiritually, and emotionally and the skill to translate and simplify certain realities in terms they can understand. But we also need courage to lean in and engage with them on the important matters of the heart. They are sponges on a constant learning journey, taking in the world and trying to make sense of it and who they are in it. There are many sources of information and authority out there ready to disciple them in a version of reality that is vastly different from the one we want them to embrace. If we are not present and engaged in the conversation around whatever is influencing the attitudes, beliefs, affections, and desires of their hearts, we forfeit our opportunity to speak the truths we want them to hear.

Sexuality is probably one of the biggest areas many parents today feel completely intimidated about discussing with their kids. However, we are also seeing what happens when kids grow up with Christian parents who either stay silent about sex or address it in a way that either brings shame or just doesn't capture their hearts—they are unprepared to face both the internal and external battle over sexuality that none of us can avoid. We live in a society in which it is almost impossible to filter out the constant bombardment of a godless, anti-biblical, and anti-human sexual value system and agenda that permeates our culture, from social media to pornography to Hollywood to public education from kindergarten through university. Sadly, so many parents today have been blindsided by this culture's aggressive plan to convert their children and are watching, heartbroken, as their kids fall prey to destructive ideology and behavior. The lesson is clear—we must have a plan to train our children to face what the enemy will throw at them. Jesus told us to be "wise as serpents and innocent as doves," which means that we understand how the enemy operates while aligning our hearts and lives with how God operates. Raising wise and innocent children cannot happen by keeping them ignorant of the truth. We must tell them both the truth of God's beautiful and powerful design for our sexuality and the truth of the destruction that invariably follows when we step outside that design.

When Delani was nine, she came home from school one day and told us that a boy in her class kept telling her he wanted to "sext" her. Ben and I looked at each other in a slight panic. Up to this point, the most we had told her about sex was that it was where babies come from—"Mommy and Daddy 'make love' and that's how we get a baby." But now we both knew it was time to have a *real* sex talk with our daughter.

I asked Delani if she wanted to go for a ride to the local drugstore or go for a walk by the cows. She picked the drugstore, because she knew there was a much greater chance of me buying her a treat there. I also asked her if she wanted Daddy to be part of the sex conversation, and she said she just wanted it to be us girls. So we left for the drugstore, and in the car I asked her, "So what does it mean to have sex with someone?"

"Well, it's when a mommy and daddy lie on the couch, kiss a lot, and then the couch turns red," she answered. "This means they have had love."

I was not prepared for that! I knew she didn't know much, but I had to try not to laugh at the innocence of her response. Obviously I had a lot to fill her in on. I began by giving her a basic overview of sexual intercourse and conception, and then explained why these belong in a lifelong relationship with a husband and wife in the covenant of marriage.

By the time I finished, we had been sitting in the drugstore parking lot for ten minutes. I asked her how she was feeling and if she had any questions. She said she was good and wanted to go inside. A few minutes later, as we were walking down an aisle looking for nail polish, she asked, "So, Mom, when the penis gets really big and ejaculates the white stuff, that stuff is what you need to help make the babies, right?"

Of course, we had to be standing near about four other people when she asked this question, and I could just *feel* them wondering what in the world sparked this question and how I was going to respond. I realized I could respond with embarrassment and tell her we would talk about it later, or choose to protect the freedom and safety in talking about this subject I wanted to build with my daughter. So I replied, "Yes, that is correct. The white stuff that comes out is called sperm. You need an egg from the mommy and the sperm from the daddy to make a baby. Did you find a color of polish that you wanted?"

After we left the store I explained to Delani that it's better to ask sex questions when there aren't a bunch of strangers around, because not everyone is as comfortable discussing the topic. But I also told her I was so happy that she didn't feel scared to ask me that question, no matter who was there! In the years since, we have had many more conversations as

Delani has matured into a young woman and encountered more cultural realities. Some of these have been very difficult, but through it all I have continued to fight to create a place where she can discuss and ask questions freely.

With both Delani and Adalyn, it was more natural to discuss sex from a female perspective, and for a long time I assumed that I would handle the sex talks with them and Ben could handle it with Lincoln. Then I read *Strong Mothers, Strong Sons* by Dr. Meg Meeker, who explains why it is important that mothers speak to their sons about sexuality, and specifically how they ought to view women, ideally before they turned twelve. Soon after reading this, I came into the living room one day and found Lincoln watching something on an iPad.

"Hey, bud, what are you doing?" I asked him curiously.

"Watching a YouTube video about Fortnite. When can I play this?"

Despite Fortnite being the most popular video game that many of his friends and peers were playing, and despite him making multiple requests to play it, we hadn't yet let him do so and hadn't explained why. Feeling nudged by the book I had just read and maybe the Holy Spirit, I decided to invite him into a conversation. I sat down beside him, looked him in the eye, and said, "Here's the thing, buddy. I know you want to play this game and that your friends play it. But I'm not going to parent any of them, only you. And for Mommy's heart, Fortnite just feels a little scary and I feel like you're not supposed to play it yet. I don't know when you'll get to play it—maybe one day. But part of why I don't think it's the right time is that in Fortnite, they have these girls who look sexy. And the more you let in these sexy images, the more you think that's normal. And if that becomes normal, then it's easier to think it's normal to interact with or touch a girl who looks sexy—not just in video games, but in real life."

Lincoln was looking down, but I could tell he was listening with rapt attention, so I continued.

"Whatever you let in your head affects your heart, and that affects your parts. You've talked to Daddy about that, right?"

"Yeah."

"So I want you to do a really good job of protecting your head because it protects all the other things. Someday you're going to get married and have a wife. Can you imagine if Daddy looked at sexy girls? How would that make me feel? How would that make you feel?"

Without hesitation, he said, "I would feel so mad."

"Right? So I need to help you learn how to protect your head right now from those sexy images so that you don't ever go looking for them. Because they will never make you feel good and they will never make your wife feel good. And that's why I'm saying no to Fortnite right now and might say no to other things. I'm going to help you protect your wife. Do you want to help protect her with me?"

He nodded. "Yes, I do."

"Awesome." I then changed the subject and suggested that he help clean the kitchen to show appreciation for his sisters, who had made food for him earlier that day. He jumped up to go do it, but after a few steps he stopped, turned around, and said, "Thanks for talking to me, Mom."

"You're welcome, buddy. I love you." As soon as he had left the room, I burst into tears. I couldn't believe he had thanked me for having a conversation about sex and, essentially, porn. Now Ben and I could be a united front for him to talk about these topics.

As it happened, it wasn't long before we had another opportunity to speak to Lincoln about his head, heart, and parts. We were all at home watching a movie on the couch, and out of the blue, Lincoln put Adalyn's foot over his crotch and rubbed against it. She immediately flipped out. Ben and I decided to have everyone calm down and finish the show before addressing it. The girls went upstairs to bed and Ben and I stayed on the couch with Lincoln.

"So can you tell us what you were doing and why?" Ben asked him. "Why would you think that's okay to do to your sister?"

"I don't know. I just did it," Lincoln answered, his head hanging in shame. "I kind of thought it would be funny and wanted to see what would happen."

"Did something happen?" I asked him. "Did you see something that maybe got into your head?"

"I saw a yucky photo today on Dad's phone when I was playing a game," he said. "An ad popped up. I put the phone down fast so Dad wouldn't see."

"Was this at church?" Ben asked.

"Yeah."

"I remember you doing that and wondered what was going on," Ben said.

"Remember how we talked about your head, your heart, and your parts?" I asked.

Lincoln nodded.

"This is what happened. Something got in your head, started messing with your heart, and it's chasing after your parts. And that thing also wanted to tell you that you should hide it. But you should never hide it, even if you look at it on purpose. Because it will just make you feel more and more yucky. Come and tell us about it, okay?"

Ben and I then both hugged Lincoln and prayed for him, asking that God would protect his mind and his purity, and that Jesus would come and delete that image from his mind forever. Then I turned his face toward me, looked in his eyes, and said, "You're a good boy, Lincoln. And I want you to say this: 'I'm a good boy. Jesus loves me and I'm forgiven.'"

Through tears, Lincoln repeated my words. As soon as we released him, he went upstairs, found Adalyn, and told her, "I'm sorry for not protecting you. I won't ever do that again." She forgave him, and that was that.

Ben and I both know that we're not always going to be there to nip every attack from the enemy in the bud. But we want to be paying attention and be fully engaged in whatever messages are trying to get access to our kids' hearts and shape their beliefs and desires, whether they're about sex, their identity and worth, their purpose in life, what's good and what's bad, or how to fit in and succeed in life. We want to be there to constantly speak the truth over them, and live out that truth as best we can, so they can trust our voices—the voices of the people who love and know them best—over any others. And of course, even more than that, we want them to anchor their hearts by trusting in the voice of truth Himself, which brings us to the next pillar.

THE PILLAR OF FAITH

Faith is the pillar that anchors us to the source of all the other pillars. Can you have love, honor, self-control, responsibility, trust, and vision without a close relationship with God? Yes, to a degree, but it will be a trickle, a dilution, a mixture. You won't be getting these qualities in their most unadulterated and potent form like you can when you go to the source. If Ben and I want to become the best models for our kids of what these pillars look like in action, then we know we need to go to the source and we need to teach our kids to go to the source.

This obviously includes practicing spiritual disciplines in front of them and teaching them to practice them as well—reading and meditating on Scripture, prayer, worship, small groups or Bible studies, weekly church meetings, Sunday school, giving, Sabbath, and more. This doesn't mean that we are showing off our relationship with God—each of us parents still needs a devotional life in the secret place with the Lord—but it does mean that relationship is not a secret. We are actively pursuing Him as our source—this is the whole point of all spiritual disciplines!

Now let's be real, for most of us, our pursuit of God while juggling marriage, kids, a home, jobs, church, and everything else doesn't look like the disciplined, serene, monk-like lifestyle we often envision as the ideal for our spiritual lives. We don't get to rise early, study Scripture and pray for two hours, and step into our days full of boundless peace. I remember, in my childless youth, that there was a season of a few years in which I had the luxury of doing something like that, but as soon as Delani came along, I was humbled to discover that I no longer had the time or energy to knock out daily Bible study morning and evening. So I had to learn what the Lord was asking of me in each season. Whatever it was, there was grace for it, but it also required me to be intentional and sacrificial about prioritizing time for Him. Some days, that time has looked like blasting worship music in the car for ten minutes while I'm waiting to pick up my kids or listening to Scripture in one Airpod while feeding my child cereal. There have also been plenty of times when I've realized that I've been neglecting Him. I like to use the analogy of the car dashboard with the lights that pop on to tell you something's going on under the hood. You need more oil, more gas, more coolant, more air in your tires. Our spiritual dashboards start to light up when we're no longer drawing on God and His grace, as evidenced by decreased levels of the fruit of the Spirit and elevated levels of fear and anxiety, anger and frustration, discouragement and hopelessness, distraction and numbing out. These are the moments when you need to repent and go back and take a nice long drink from the source. The beauty and faithfulness of God is that He is always there to embrace us and restore us with His love and compassion, without any condemnation.

One of Ben's and my desires is to help our kids develop a love for and personal connection with Scripture. When the kids were old enough, we started doing family devotions together, and once my girls began to reach adolescence, I began to tell them how they reminded me of different women in the Bible. I explained that I saw Delani as an Esther, a woman who would be positioned in places of influence and called to stand up in boldness when at the Lord's word. I told Adalyn I saw her as a Ruth, a woman with an incredible ability to serve and lay her life down out of beautiful love and loyalty. I found some devotionals specifically on these books for us to go through, and they have both been much more engaged with them because they're looking for how these stories can offer wisdom for them personally.

But even more than introducing our kids to the Bible, we are passionate about them coming to know and encounter the God of the Bible in their daily lives. There is nothing that builds the pillar of faith like a testimony of seeing God show up in your family in real time.

THE WINNING TICKETS

One of our favorite family testimonies happened soon after we moved to Sacramento. Lincoln was in preschool at the time, and one day I spotted a notice on his classroom door advertising a "family fun fair." Being new to the area, we were always searching for cheap and entertaining things we could do with the kids, so I jumped at this opportunity. When we arrived at the fair, however, it was not what we had hoped or expected. There were no rides, bouncy houses, or funnel cakes. It was essentially a business fair with hundreds of booths where dentists, chiropractors, fitness gyms, and all manner of salespeople could advertise their goods and services to families. Some of the booths gave out candy or had little games you could play to win a prize, but most of them were offering flyers or business-related products like little baggies with a toothbrush and toothpaste.

Figuring that we might as well walk around the fair for a little while, we explored the booths and soon came to one advertising a country radio station called The Bull. As we passed by the display, the person behind the table said, "Hey, do you guys want to take a photo? We're doing a giveaway for Disneyland."

The kids immediately perked up. "Sure, why not?" I agreed.

After we took a family photo with the booth display, the person said, "All you need to do to win is post the picture on Facebook, tag us, and whoever has the most likes by the end of the next seventy-two hours wins two tickets to Disneyland."

Well, I had no illusion that we were going to win anything, but the kids were so excited that I couldn't help indulging them by posting the photo and asking for likes. After that we moved on and spent the next hour or two collecting candy, toothbrushes, magnets, and other random promotional goodies, and actually had a lot of fun in the end, despite it not being the fair we had imagined.

I would have completely forgotten about the photo on Facebook had my kids not reminded me. When I checked it a few days after the fair, I was shocked to see the number of people who had liked it and shared it for other people to like. Not too many days later, I got a voicemail message from The Bull radio station saying, "Congratulations! You won the Disneyland tickets!"

After my initial shock, the first emotion I felt was irritation. What were we going to do with two tickets to Disneyland? We couldn't afford to buy three more, plus cover travel and lodging. Then, when I tried to discuss this dilemma with Ben, I apparently didn't do a very good job of keeping the conversation private, because our kids, who are highly skilled at listening when they're not supposed to be listening, figured out what was going on and immediately exploded with excitement. "We won!" So then we had to figure out how to bring them back down to earth.

I took my usual approach, which was to pull no punches. "Yes, we won, which is exciting. But this is the deal, guys. I don't think that we should take the tickets."

"What?!"

"Well, there are two tickets. How many people are in our family?"

"Five."

"So winning two tickets to Disneyland for one day is like me giving you fifty cents and saying, go ahead and go to the dollar store and buy what you want. You're going to look at everything and get nothing. The only way we could possibly afford to pay for three more tickets and gas and food and a hotel for all of us is if we all give up going to the movie theater, eating out after church, and all the other treats we like to enjoy for about a year."

Immediately, all three of them jumped at this "chance" I was giving them. "Yes, we can do that!"

My first thought was, *Liars! You are all liars!* I knew they couldn't and wouldn't succeed at making this year-long sacrifice. The loss of short-term rewards would soon eclipse the big reward they were hoping for, and it would fall on Ben's and my shoulders to calm their whining about why we couldn't go to Red Robin after church and remind them that they had chosen this. No, thank you!

Thankfully, Ben stepped in at this point and started talking about how wonderful it is to be generous. He pointed out that the family who had won second place in the contest consisted of two parents and a son who was still young enough to get free admission to Disneyland. They could take the two tickets and enjoy the trip much more easily than we could. He went on to exhort them that God blesses us when we live generously and loves when we position our heart to receive because we've made room for more by giving away.

After this beautiful little sermon, which I could see had clearly had an effect on the kids, I said, "Okay, let's do a family vote. Do we spend the next year sacrificing so we can get the extra tickets we need, or do we practice generosity and align with God's heart?" (Yes, I admit I was a little manipulative in this description.)

So everyone wrote down their vote on a piece of paper. Delani offered to write Lincoln's for him, but I stepped in to prevent this and did it for him myself. We then collected the votes in a brown paper bag and I shook it for dramatic effect. I already knew what Ben, Lincoln, and I had voted for, and I thought I could guess what the girls had written based on the way they were sitting there in excited anticipation.

The first piece of paper I pulled out said, "Give away."

The next one read, "Keep."

The third one said, "Give away.

The fourth said, "Keep."

There we were, a house divided, waiting with bated breath to see the tie breaker. The tension in the room had reached an incredible height. Delani was sitting on the edge of her seat, biting her nails.

I was completely sure that the last piece of paper would say, "Keep," because I knew the two "Give aways" were from Ben and me, and one of the "Keeps" was from Lincoln. I felt sure both girls also wanted to keep the tickets. But to my utter shock, when I pulled out the paper, it read, "Give away." I looked at Ben in shock, and then at the girls, who simultaneously burst into tears. I couldn't ask them which ones were their votes, because in a few moments Delani was crying on the floor (she does this a lot) and Adalyn was kneeling beside her trying to comfort her.

Ben joined them and again spoke like a good dad, reminding them that this was just one situation, one opportunity, and there would be others. We had made the decision as a family. We had made a way for God to bless us, and we were going to trust Him to do that. We were not going to believe that He was not good. He had heard the desires of our hearts and we were gonna thank Him for the opportunity to bless our family.

Meanwhile, I had already pulled out my phone to write back to The Bull. I explained that we appreciated the tickets, but we were a bigger family and felt that the runners-up in the contest could use the tickets more, so we'd appreciate it if the station just gave them to them. I then put my phone down and returned to soothing the raw and disappointed hearts of my kids.

Fifteen or twenty minutes later, I heard my phone buzz. I went over and picked it up, opened the new text, and couldn't believe what I was reading. I looked at Ben and nodded for him to come over. After reading the text again to doublecheck I had understood it correctly, I handed it to him. His face quickly assumed the same shocked look I guessed I must be wearing. The message said that the contest organizers were so blown away that we would give up the Disney tickets that they had gone and found four Disneyland tickets, for two days, that they wanted to give us.

It was an incredible turn of events, but it still created a dilemma, because we would need to cover a fifth two-day ticket and expenses. Ben and I silently agreed not to say anything to the kids in that moment. We got them squared away watching a movie and then went to find my dad in his office.

"Yoda, can we talk to you?" we asked. (This is our favorite name for him when we want him to step in as our life and relationship guru.)

"Sure!"

We told him the whole story and then I said, "What do we do? Do we take these tickets?"

"Well, what's the problem?" he asked.

I've always hated when my dad asks me this question, because it means I thought I knew what the problem was, but apparently I've missed it. So I quickly reviewed everything in my mind and said, "Well, I mean, we're trying to teach the kids about generosity."

"Oh," he replied. "I thought you were trying to teach them about God's love."

Conviction hit me. I was putting God in a box and resisting letting Him love my kids in the way He seemed to be doing because I didn't want the work that came with it. I had become so set on what I wanted them to learn, not what He wanted them to learn, that I was ready to turn down four two-day Disneyland tickets. Apparently Ben was thinking something similar, because we both started laughing in slight embarrassment. My dad started laughing at us too.

After we had finished laughing at ourselves, we went back to tell the kids the news. Ben started in with, "So you know how we were saying that God is good and He knows the desires of our hearts? Well, sometimes when we choose to be generous, He decides to turn around and bless us faster than we were expecting." I then read them the text message from the radio station.

You would have thought we told them we had just won a million dollars on the big wheel spin on *Wheel of Fortune*. They absolutely lost their minds. It was so hilarious and delightful to see them jumping around the room in high rapture.

The beautiful thing about the situation was that along with the lesson about generosity and God's love, we also got to teach our kids about sacrifice and saving for something they wanted. We didn't have to give up treats for a year, but we started a Disneyland fund jar to throw all our extra money in. I remember one day Lincoln found a quarter while we were on a walk and carried it all the way home and put it in the Disneyland jar. Our friends found out about the story of the tickets and our jar, and many of them randomly gave us cash or presented us with $25 gift cards to the Disney store. When the jar was full, we picked out days for the trip, booked our hotels, and in highest anticipation, drove from Sacramento to Anaheim for our great adventure. As an added treat, Ben's parents decided to join us for the trip, which made it extra special for both them and us. Everyone had the time of their lives. It was truly an unforgettable experience and a core memory for all of us—not just because it was Disneyland, but because it was an encounter with God's love for our whole family.

My favorite thing about this story is that it was one of pure grace. Ben and I didn't get to take credit for our amazing faith or parenting and character skills. It was a clear instance of the Lord saying, "You think you got this one? Let Me one-up you. Let Me show you My goodness, love, and care for you." And He gave us a testimony that we now carry as a family that reminds us that some impossible things are possible.

PARENTING WITH THE HOLY SPIRIT

One of the great reminders that the Disneyland episode and many other testimonies give Ben and me is that the Lord wants to partner with us in all things, including our parenting. We are not just His servants or employees trying to figure things out the best we can. He is available and right there in the midst of it all with us, ready to bring wisdom, discernment, hope, courage, strength, and every other resource we need to love and lead our kids with His love. The challenge is always continuing to surrender our agenda and desires and seeking to align our hearts and behavior with His agenda and heart. This is the test of our faith, and as we know, faith can't grow without testing.

When Delani reached seventh grade, she began to experience a series of tests and struggles that also became tests for us as her parents. Her first big struggle was with her education. She had an IEP (individual education plan) to help her succeed but still found herself experiencing some disappointing and demoralizing failures. These are tough at any age, but they can be especially difficult when you're twelve and insecure and trying to figure out your worth and identity. We did our best to encourage her, empathize with her, and champion her, but we couldn't be there to chase away every lie pounding at her door.

One of the metaphors I like to use to describe parenting is that it's like teaching someone to sail a boat. You start by having the person in your own boat watching you, then you have them join in performing various tasks. Eventually they get their own boat, but you keep a rope tethered to them so you can pull them back and keep them from getting pulled out of the safe, warm bay and out on the open seas too early. Well, by this point, Delani was in her own boat, and she was starting to try to untie that rope tethering us. This looked like getting snippy and short with us, becoming more moody and withdrawn, and spending more time on her phone, which we soon took away from her. We did our best to engage her in conversation and try to find out what was going on with her. When she did open up about things, we were surprised to learn that not only was she dealing with her academic anxieties, but she had also somehow become caught up in various friend dramas and was investing huge amounts of emotional energy in them. This wasn't the first time that we had observed that Delani is a deep feeler with a huge heart of compassion for people. We tried to be positive in affirming this gift and capacity in her, while also urging her that it was something she needed to learn to steward and set boundaries with, or she would find herself sinking under the weight of her emotions and care for people.

Well, in the midst of all this there was one week where Delani seemed to be extra edgy, emotional, and irritable. Every little thing seemed to be a cause for arguing and disrespectful comments. One particular evening, the issue was her phone—she was mad that we had taken it away from her and was complaining that we didn't understand her and the whole thing was so ridiculous (teenagers!). I was communicating that she could have it as soon as we felt like she could manage to protect and prioritize our relationship over the attention she was giving her phone. I did a pretty good job staying calm and using the one-liners with her—"Probably so. I know. That could be"—but after twenty or thirty minutes of listening to her frustrated griping, I was done. It was ten in the evening, so I said, "Well, it's time for bed. I would be happy to finish the conversation in the morning, okay?" I patted her, said good night, and left the room.

Back in my room as I started getting in my pajamas, I was stewing in my own frustration. What was going on with my daughter? Why did we keep getting tripped up by this cycle of conflict and disconnection? Why couldn't we figure out what the problem was?

Then I heard the inner voice of the Holy Spirit interrupting my thoughts. *Go back in Delani's room.*

I really did not want to go back in that room. I knew it was just going to be another round of being a punching bag. I was exhausted and didn't feel like I had the energy to manage myself in the presence of her attitude. But then I heard it again. *Go back in her room . . . Do you trust Me?*

Okay, Lord, I hear You. I trust You.

I headed back to Delani's room, and when I opened her door I saw the last thing I expected to see. My daughter was holding a pair of scissors and rubbing the blade against her naked forearm near her wrist. She was clearly attempting to cut herself.

She looked up at me, and I can only conclude that the Holy Spirit gave me supernatural calm, because I didn't start freaking out. Instead, I said, "Well, that's not a very good idea. What are you doing, honey?"

She looked at me defiantly and said, "I'm cutting myself."

"I can see that. I don't think that's a very good idea." I walked over to her with my hand out. "Let me have the scissors."

Just then, Ben entered the room. "What's going on?"

I looked at him and said, "Well, your daughter has decided that cutting herself is a good option."

Now, Ben hardly ever gets riled—certainly far less often than I do, and it's always much milder when it happens. But in this moment, his protective fatherly anger hit a new high and he immediately looked at Delani with horror. "What are you doing?!"

Delani's defiant look evaporated, and she handed me the scissors.

"I don't think you're going to be able to stay in your room tonight," I told her.

"What is your *deal*?" she protested. "Why are you trying to control me? You're always doing this!"

"Probably so," I responded. "Go ahead and grab your pillow and a blanket, and follow me."

She reluctantly obeyed and followed Ben and me back to our bedroom. Ben was actually following me too, because he didn't have any idea what was going on. Frankly, I didn't either, but what I did have was this tremendous sense of peace. On one level it felt like I was improvising this whole thing, but in my spirit I felt like I was simply following a yellow brick road the Holy Spirit had laid out before me, because it was just easy. I didn't have any desire to question the steps I was taking—I felt confident they were being guided.

I shut the door to our room and turned to Delani. "Honey, I'm not sure what you're needing. I'm not sure what you're looking for. But this is not who you are. I just want to let you know that it's obvious to me that you are fighting with a lie that wants to take root. This lie says, 'Don't trust your parents. Don't let them in. They don't understand you and they will never be there for you. They don't actually love you.' I think that lie feels really loud. But the truth is, we love you more than any other thing in this world. We want to understand you, we want to be supportive, and we want to be there for you. That is the truth. And tonight, you are faced with the choice to partner with the truth or a lie. It's your decision. I cannot make this decision for you. I cannot fight this battle for you. I can never find what your lies are and rip them out. This is something you will have to do without me. But tonight, I'm going to ask that you sleep in our bed. If you do, I feel that you will be choosing to partner with the truth. If you don't want to, that's okay. You can sleep on the floor. But if you do that, I think you'll be choosing to partner with the lie. We love you. Where are you going to sleep?"

Delani was staring at me with a look of utter disgust that could kill. But after a moment, she said, "Well, don't touch me." Then she climbed up in our bed.

I looked at Ben and said, "Okay, let's go to bed." We quickly got ready and laid down on either side of Delani. Lying there, I had the sense that we had just entered the first battle in a season of warring for our daughter's heart and life. I didn't know how this battle would end, how many battles lay ahead for us, or how long the warring season would last. But something had shifted and there was no going back to a previous simpler time.

Neither Ben nor I was touching Lani, per her request. But I said, "Lani, I'm gonna play a song for you. I believe the lyrics to be true for you, and if you could just listen, that's all I need you to do."

Delani didn't say anything. I found the song "Breakthrough" by Chris McClarney and turned it on.

There must be more
Beyond familiar shores

Into waters unexplored
This one desire
Stirring here in me
Deep is calling out to deep
Take me from where I've been
Into something new
I'm giving up control
I need a breakthrough
All of my dreams and fears
Are crashing into You
You're waking up my hope
You are my breakthrough
Come breakthrough

Your love, so wild
Conquers my defense
Opens the impossible
It's so amazing
How You take the ashes
And turn them into beautiful

You're making all things new
You're making all things new
It's what You always do
You are my breakthrough[4]

As this declaration rang out over us in the darkness, Ben and I lay like walls on either side of our daughter, silently weeping and praying for these words to penetrate her heart. It felt like we were putting a stake in the ground

---

[4] Chris McClarney, "Breakthrough." Track 6 on *Breakthrough*. Jesus Culture under exclusive license to Capitol Christian Music Group, Inc, 2018. Digital track.

and showing her that no matter what she did or which painful choices she made, we were going to continue to pursue her.

We had no idea that our warring season with Delani, which I'll describe more fully in Chapter 10, would last another two years. But I am eternally grateful that right from the beginning, the Holy Spirit showed up and made it very clear that He wanted to partner with us as we navigated these uncharted waters. We encountered many moments when we felt shocked, blindsided, overwhelmed, grieved, furious, discouraged, confused, and at a loss to know what to do. Yet in every one of these situations, we found our way back to peace, hope, and strength by remembering we were not alone. The Holy Spirit, our Partner in parenting, was never blindsided, never freaking out, never overwhelmed, and always knew what to do. Our job was to lean into Him, regulate our hearts with His presence, love, and truth, and then engage fully with our daughter from His posture of total calm in the storm. All we had to do was love her and show her that we were not letting go of our end of the rope, no matter how hard she tried to shake us off.

Establishing the pillar of faith is so critical in our families because it's like a compass that constantly brings us back to true north—not just in parenting or in marriage, but in our whole lives. Jesus came with one purpose—to show us the Father. Our purpose is first to know and walk with the Father through the Holy Spirit, and then to show Him to those around us. Eugene Peterson, author of *The Message* paraphrase of the Bible, passed away in 2018. At his memorial, his son, Leif, said that though his father had preached thousands of sermons, he really only had one message, which he had whispered every night to his son: "God loves you. He's on your side. He's coming after you. He's relentless." This is the heart of the Father for us, and this is what we need to believe and show to our kids. Because eventually, they will sail their boats out onto the open sea. And what will keep them afloat is not being tied to us but being tied to Him.

So those are the pillars of trust and faith. We build these by:

- Being careful not to send mixed messages
- Using few words combined with meaningful actions
- Telling our kids the truth, especially about important topics like sexuality
- Making time to nurture connection with the Holy Spirit and practice spiritual disciplines
- Allowing God to surprise us with miracles and encounters that reveal His power and character to our kids
- Allowing the Holy Spirit to lead us in tough parenting moments

8

The Structure of Connection: Vision

IN 1952, FLORENCE MAY CHADWICK, the first female swimmer to swim the English Channel in both directions, attempted a new feat—swimming out to Catalina Island from the California coast. A few people in small boats accompanied her as she made the twenty-six mile journey, looking out for sharks and ready to offer support if she needed it. After fifteen hours of swimming, a thick fog descended on the water, blocking her view of Catalina Island. Without visibility, Florence began to feel disoriented, unsure of the remaining distance, and insecure in her ability to complete the swim. After another hour, she called out to the people in the boats and asked to be pulled out of the water, thereby ending her swim. As she sat resting in the boats, someone told her that they were only one mile from the Catalina coast. She had swum twenty-five miles and stopped just short of her goal!

Two months later, Florence decided to attempt the swim to Catalina Island for a second time. Yet again, as she came within a few miles of the coast, a thick fog set in and blocked her view. This time, however, she kept an image of the shoreline in her mind as she swam. This mental vision kept her from questioning herself. She successfully completed her journey and achieved her goal—a feat she would go on to perform two more times!

This is the power of vision—it reframes our current difficulties and struggles in a way that orients us to push forward, rather than fall back into doubt and confusion. When the pillar of vision is strong in our relationships, we have a mental image of where we're trying to go that we can hold on to, even when the fog of fear, chaos, conflict, and disconnection descends and tries to discourage us. Specifically, we have a vision for who we are going to be, what we are going to do, and the goals we are going to pursue, no matter the situation.

Proverbs 29:18 says, "Where there is no vision, the people perish" (KJV). Another translation says, "Where there is no prophetic vision, the people cast off restraint" (NKJV). The vision we need is not something we just come up with on our own. It is actually a divinely inspired vision, a revelation of who God is, who He is calling us to be, and where He is leading us. Without receiving this revelation for our lives, we "cast off restraint"— the word in Hebrew means to let the reins go. Without the vision of God for our lives, it's like we're riding a runaway horse with no way of stopping it. It is not going to end well for us. But with that vision, we are able to harness the energy and resources He's given us and use them to get us where we need to go. Vision makes us powerful. And powerful is who we need to be if we are going to stay fully engaged in this messy, challenging, at times painful and even excruciating, yet utterly rewarding process of overcoming fear and winning the war of connection in our relationships and families— and raising our kids to fight that war themselves.

LINCOLN'S TAEKWONDO JOURNEY

One of Ben's and my favorite examples of where we're seeing our kids discover the power of vision in their lives is Lincoln's journey with taekwondo, which he began at eight years old. He immediately fell in love with it and constantly practiced his fighting moves at home. He had never displayed that level of interest or passion in any other sport, so we knew we had found the right one for him.

If you're not familiar with this martial art, you start as a white belt and then progress to orange, yellow, camouflage or "low" green, green, purple, blue, brown, red, and black. Until you get to your low green belt, the sport is no contact—you're just learning the concepts and form for each fighting move. Once you earn your low green belt, however, you start learning to spar with other people. At Lincoln's studio, the low green belts are called "fresh meat" because they are brand new to fighting, and everyone is supposed to know to be gentler with them as they learn. Sparring at this level isn't supposed to be true fighting—it's more about practicing your kicks and punches with an actual person.

As soon as Lincoln got his low green belt, we got him his sparring gear—a helmet, mouthguard, foot and fist pads, and athletic cup. Even with this protection, he was admittedly terrified to get on the sparring mat. The instructor divided the class into pairs and explained that each pair would spar until he gave the command to stop, at which point they were to bow to each other and then rotate around the room to the next partner so that they would get to spar with each person in the class.

Lincoln's first partner was a boy we had watched in the class for some time. He was a little more advanced than Lincoln, but the problem was that he was not very self-aware or in control of the level of intensity he was bringing in his fighting moves. The instructor gave the command to start, and Lincoln managed to hold his own until he heard the command to stop, then obediently dropped his blocking position and prepared to bow. Unfortunately, however, the boy he was fighting had apparently not heard the command and delivered a kick directly to Lincoln's groin. Lincoln immediately collapsed to the ground in tears. The boy rushed over to apologize, but Lincoln continued to lie there, balled up and crying. Ben wasn't there, so I stepped in to comfort him and try to help him recover. Without diminishing his physical pain, I suspected that his tears were as much due to embarrassment, anger, and frustration at the other boy for not following the rules and playing fair.

At each of Lincoln's next few sparring classes, he was again caught off guard by rogue punches and kicks and ended up in tears, and I could tell that Lincoln's dislike and fear of sparring were growing rapidly. The instructors had warned the "fresh meat" parents that there were going to be lots of tears, but I began to wonder how we were to gauge what was "a lot" and what was too much. When should I push him, and when should I protect him? At home he continued to practice with his best friend, so I knew he still cared about trying to succeed at his sport. Yet now his confidence began to drop as soon as we arrived at the studio for his next sparring lesson.

One day before I drove him to class, Lincoln started complaining that his tummy hurt and he didn't want to go. I said I bet his tummy was okay enough to go to class, but he insisted. I then explained that we had financially invested quite a bit in him learning taekwondo. I had just signed an eight-month contract with the studio and purchased all his sparring gear. We had also paid fees each time he tested to advance to the next belt. We had made that commitment for him, and we needed him to keep his end of the commitment by going to class. So, reluctantly, he got in the car with me. However, when we got to the studio, he flatly refused to get out of the car and go inside. I was surprised, because this was very out of character for him—I had never seen him display that level of stubborn disobedience. I was also frustrated because I didn't know what to do. I knew that either trying to hype him up or shame him into going into class would only be manipulative and counterproductive. I couldn't fight his fear for him. He had to want to fight it for himself, and the only way he would do that was by getting a vision of what could lie on the other side of him learning to master sparring. At that point, all he could see was that going into class meant getting kicked in the face again.

I had brought some eggs from our chickens for the instructor, so I said, "I need to give these eggs to Miss Jones." I grabbed the eggs, left him in the car, and walked to the door, wracking my brain for a way to resolve this situation.

Miss Jones met me by the door and immediately asked, "Where's Lincoln?"

"He's in the car. He doesn't want to come in."

"Why?"

"Well, the last three times he's done sparring, he's gotten hurt."

"The last three times?" She looked surprised. Then she said, "Well, that's my fault."

"How is it your fault?" I asked.

"It's my job to make sure these guys feel safe," she explained. "I have clearly not done that if he keeps getting hurt."

"Would you mind coming and telling him that?" I asked, feeling hopeful. "I can't get him out of the car and I don't want to drag him in here."

"Of course."

So Miss Jones, barefoot in her uniform, came out to the car and opened the door to reveal a teary-eyed Lincoln. "Your mom told me you got hurt the last three times," she said to him.

"Yeah."

"Well, it's my job to help protect you, and I'm sorry I didn't pay closer attention," she said sincerely. "I'm going to stand next to you while you're sparring today, and I will protect you. The point of sparring is to teach you how not to get hurt. Do you think you could give it another try? Because I think you're really good at it."

I managed to keep a straight face, but inside I was doing a happy dance as Lincoln got out of the car and followed Miss Jones inside. Sure enough, she kept a close eye on Lincoln throughout the class, and this time he had a completely different experience. He didn't get hurt, and he started to learn how to better protect himself.

Apparently Miss Jones passed the memo on to the other instructors, because they all began to pay more attention to Lincoln over the next few weeks and help him start to fill the gaps in his sparring skills. With each class, his confidence grew as he began to understand the purpose behind each of the moves he was practicing and how to use them effectively.

On the first day of Lincoln's sparring classes, the instructors had announced that there was a sparring tournament with kids from other studios coming up in a few months, and they wanted everyone in the class to sign up for it. Competing in a certain number of tournaments is required for anyone who wants to advance to black belt. One instructor explained that she didn't spar in a tournament until she was a purple belt, and it was much scarier because everyone at that level was much bigger, stronger, and more skilled, so she highly encouraged all the green belts to start competing in tournaments right away. After the first few disastrous sparring classes, I thought there was no way Lincoln would enter a tournament, but after the turning point with Miss Jones and improving his skills for a few weeks, he got the courage to sign up for it. I was so proud of him!

However, when the tournament arrived, I admit I was feeling nervous. I knew this was going to be another big test, not only of Lincoln's skill, but of his resolve and commitment to taekwondo in particular, and to doing hard and potentially painful things in general. The first event in the tournament was a test of form. Lincoln placed second. It was so enjoyable to watch him perform the moves with such accuracy—it almost looked like he was dancing.

The next event was sparring. They had all the participants assigned to one of eight mats by age group rather than belt level, so the other kids at Lincoln's mat wore many different colored belts. They called Lincoln's name first and then his opponent, an unknown boy from another studio wearing a red belt, who we later learned had apparently already been recommended as a black belt. It was like a matchup of David and Goliath.

Our entire family was posted on three corners of the mat. My dad occupied one corner with his phone out, filming, Ben and Adalyn were on another corner (she had my phone and was also filming), and Delani, my mom, and I were gripping each other on the third corner, white-knuckled, looking like we were about to watch a gladiator fight to the death.

As soon as the referee called the start, Lincoln immediately did exactly what he had been practicing in his training. He stayed "bladed," which means he had his backside swiveled to face his opponent with his fists lined up in a defensive position, fully guarding his chest. Then he let out the loudest "kihap" (the yell you use in taekwondo when punching or kicking) I had ever heard from him and began to fight. I couldn't help grinning seeing him in full Jackie Chan mode. In taekwondo, each sparring round is three minutes long, and the competitors get points for landing kicks to each other's chest protectors and padded helmets. After each point is scored, the fighters reset and begin again. Well, Lincoln stayed in full fight mode the entire round, despite taking a few kicks to the chest. He succeeded in landing several kicks to his opponent and ended up winning the round!

Lincoln's second fight was against one of his friends, and he lost, but he still performed well. In the end, he won third place in sparring. We were all so proud of him! We went out to lunch afterwards as a family, and Lincoln wore his medals the whole time. As we celebrated, I marveled at the change in him. We had gone from him in tears and refusing to get out of the car because he was so afraid of sparring to winning third place in a sparring tournament in just a few months—all because he had caught a vision of himself learning the skills to be successful.

Lincoln has continued to improve in his sparring skills, as well as breaking boards with punches and kicks. He's had more painful moments—in one sparring match with a boy three years older and much taller than him, he took a punch straight to the nose—but he has responded to these completely differently than he did to those first few injuries, because now he knows what to do. He knows he has the skills to protect himself and he has continued to get out there and compete, both in his training and in further tournaments. He has clung to the vision of success that Miss Jones helped him grab on to in his most fearful moment, and his commitment to that vision has only deepened as he has progressed from belt to belt. This year, he got his black belt and became a junior instructor for the kids with colored belts!

VISION IN A FAMILY

I know one of the things that has spurred Lincoln on in his journey with taekwondo is that our whole family has rallied to support him. We saw the signs that this sport is where his passion and skills come alive, so we caught the vision too and have helped him to carry it. We have been there at his tournaments, surrounding the mat, ready to cheer with him when he wins and to comfort and encourage him when he loses. It's been especially beautiful to watch his two sisters tell him that they believe in him and celebrate him pursuing his goal.

Supporting Lincoln is just one expression of the larger vision we've been developing as a family for many years. It began as a vision for our marriage, which Ben and I really grabbed on to when we had our first major turning point as a couple and shifted toward the goal of understanding, complementing, and connecting with each other. Sure, we had articulated some of this vision in our vows to love each other on our wedding day. But not until we found ourselves struggling to even like each other did we understand that we needed to take hold of a vision that had the power to help us overcome our fear and default self-protection reactions—in my case, anger and perfectionism, and in his case, going passive and having no needs—so we could actually start consistently being who we wanted to be in our relationship. Just as Lincoln had a general vision for taekwondo but only learned to grab on to it when it became scary and painful, it seems that vision is something we don't really possess until things get difficult—until we are tested.

As I mentioned in Chapter 5, our move to Sacramento was another significant test of our vision as a couple and as a family. No longer could we coast along on the support of the Bethel community. We had to figure out what our priorities, core values, expectations, and standards were, and which practices we would begin to establish in our family to teach, encourage, and enforce them. We had to build our family culture, and to do that, we needed a vision for that culture.

At the core of that vision was the same commitment Ben and I had embraced in our marriage. As a family, our goal was to pursue the goal of connection no matter what, to help each other shine in our areas of strength and to overcome their weaknesses, and to pursue love over fear and insecurity. But in that season of seeking vision, God added more revelation to our understanding of the kind and quality of connection He was calling us to build with each other. The Seven Pillars were a key concept we adopted, as I've said, and we combined this with our study of God's design for our relationships with Him, ourselves, and others, specifically our spouse and children. We began to understand that each of the Seven Pillars needs to operate in those three relational dimensions—for example, if we don't have a vision for ourselves personally, and if this vision is not being revealed and defined through our relationship with God, then we are not going to be very good at bringing a vision or helping to carry a vision for our families.

We also began to grasp the idea that our calling to become a connected family was actually part of our larger culture-building assignment in the kingdom of God. One of our favorite biblical stories emphasizing this is found in Nehemiah 4. If you're not familiar with the story, it's about the mission to rebuild the wall of Jerusalem after Judah was destroyed and its people exiled to Babylon. A city wall is a symbol of culture—the boundaries that define and protect what a society values most. Nehemiah, scribe to King Artaxerxes, was tasked with leading a remnant of settlers to complete this project. As soon as the wall began to go up, a group of neighboring tribes, who did not want to see the Jewish nation restored, started to mock, intimidate, and conspire to attack the workers. Nehemiah heard of their threats and plots, and devised a strategy to prepare the people to defend themselves without stopping the momentum of their progress on the wall:

> So I placed armed guards behind the lowest parts of the wall in the exposed areas. I stationed the people to stand guard by families, armed with swords, spears, and bows.
>
> Then as I looked over the situation, I called together the nobles and the rest of the people and said to them, "Don't be afraid of the enemy! Remember the Lord, who is great and glorious, and fight for your brothers, your sons, your daughters, your wives, and your homes!"
>
> When our enemies heard that we knew of their plans and that God had frustrated them, we all returned to our work on the wall. (Nehemiah 4:13-15 NLT)

Nehemiah understood that the best way to rouse the hearts of his people to conquer their fear was to help them fight for what they loved. He didn't tell them to fight for the wall or the city—he told them to fight for their families. He connected them to their assignment on the wall by linking it with their most important connections.

As believers, we are all called to be partners with Jesus and the body of Christ in building a culture that expresses and protects the values of His kingdom. We all have a place to work and fight on the wall, and if we don't do it, no one will! But our particular assignment in that culture-building project is connected to family, both spiritual and natural. As we learn to fight for our families, we are also learning to fight for the kingdom. It's not an exaggeration to say that the way we build our family culture affects the fate of the world. The more we grasp what's at stake in our vision, the more motivated we will be to pursue it!

THE CULTURE CREED

When you latch on to the vision of building a connected family culture, your big goal doesn't change, but the way you move toward it will adjust according to the season and stage of building you're in. When our kids were in the toddler and preschool years, our vision for building our family culture of connection focused a lot on managing ourselves well in the presence of dirty diapers, boogers, food disasters, unexpected wall art (Lincoln with my eyeshadow), tantrums, and every type of small child mess. When we moved to Sacramento, the season changed. All the kids were in school, I started working more, and Ben entered university to earn a social work degree, so our focus shifted toward how to proactively build connection and prioritize family dinner time, a family work day once a month, and family fun days in the midst of juggling multiple busy schedules, homework, friends, sports, youth group, and other activities.

One of the questions we started asking in this season was how to help our kids take more and more ownership of the family culture we were building together. Serendipitously, Ben started working on a project for school focused on helping families examine and "grade" their family culture. In the spirit of research and development, he and my dad decided to test-pilot the initial questionnaire he had written on our own family. We announced to the kids—Lani was about twelve at the time, Adalyn seven, and Lincoln five—that we were going to have a family gathering in the living room, brought a huge bowl of popcorn and another bowl of Skittles, and set up a huge whiteboard where we could write down our ideas.

My dad started off the evening by explaining to the kids what "culture" is. Ben and I soon chimed in with suggestions and we landed on two examples that really brought the concept home for them. The first was Disneyland. Our epic family trip to Disneyland was still fresh in their memories, so it was easy to get them talking about what Disneyland was like.

The streets were always clean. Every day was a happy, fun experience in that magical world. Exactly, we said, the reason there's no trash anywhere and that everyone is so friendly and fun is because that is their culture. The second example we discussed was Australia. The kids had visited their grandparents there, and they noticed how it felt different from home. There were different animals, different foods, and different things to do. Their Aussie grandparents' house was different from our house.

From there, we segued into explaining that we wanted to have a culture in our home and our family that was distinctive so that when people experienced us they would go, "That's the Serpells. That's what they're like. That's how things are done at the Serpells." So we threw out the first question to them: "What do we do well as Serpells? What is the strength of our family?"

Delani immediately said, "We love people." Adalyn echoed, "Loving on purpose." Lincoln, taking the "strength" idea literally, said, "We're good at building strong towers."

Ben and I wrote every answer down on the whiteboard and then moved on to the second question. "What is the passion of our family? What do we love to do?"

Another flood of answers began to flow. We like to go on trips, go hiking, and play outside at parks. We love having fun movie nights. We love helping people. We love Legos. And a lot more.

Third and last of all, we asked, "What are we going to be famous for?" The real question on Ben's questionnaire was "What's the legacy of our family?" but we didn't feel up for explaining the concept of legacy to them, so we simplified it and explained that by "famous," we didn't mean a YouTube or Hollywood star. What do we want people to say about us, about who we were, how they felt around us, and what we gave to people?

Once again, their answers were all over the place, but we weren't looking for perfection. We just wanted their participation in the process, and Ben and I tried to incorporate as much of what they contributed as we could in the next step, which was the much more difficult task of integrating all these answers into a simple, clear statement that expressed our strength, passion, and legacy as Serpells. We didn't do it right away that night—we turned on a funny movie and enjoyed the rest of our popcorn and Skittles laughing together. But over the next few days, Ben and I sifted through the words and phrases we had put up on the whiteboard and eventually distilled them into three simple statements:

The strength of our family is loving, helping, and protecting people.

The passion of our family is to have fun, dream big dreams, and encourage others.

Our legacy is to strengthen other families, live generously, and steward our inheritance well.

And thus, our family culture creed was born.

A week or so later, we had another family night and read these three statements to the kids. As we had anticipated, there were some phrases they didn't quite understand, such as "steward our inheritance well." So we talked about the fact that we have been given so many good things from God and from our families that we didn't earn. They're gifts for us to use, and we want to use them well. And we want to be people who are generous and give gifts to others in the same way we've been given gifts.

We discussed each statement, asked a lot of questions, and unpacked each concept until it was clear the kids were starting to grasp them. It was so much fun to see their minds and imaginations working and connecting the dots for what these core values meant for us. Even more rewarding was to see these ideas spontaneously come out of them in the weeks and months that followed. For example, we took a mini vacation to the coast, and at one point Lincoln said, "I want to come here every year." I said, "Yes, that would be nice. But we may not be able to." Then Adalyn turned around and said, "But I thought that we dreamed big dreams." I laughed and agreed.

OUR BATTLE ON THE WALL

Eventually, we had a friend of ours create a plaque with our culture creed on it, and it has hung on the wall in our living room for several years now. We all see it every day, we recite it regularly, and it frequently comes up in our conversations. However, when we formulated our culture creed, we had no idea how intensely our commitment to this vision would be tested in the next season of our lives. To be honest, Ben and I initially thought this would become a tool we would use in our coaching practice to help other families. But as we've experienced somewhat frequently, the tools we discover or build for others usually turn out to be things we need for ourselves first. This is really the grace and sovereign work of the Lord. He gives us an anchor before we head into the storm and figure out how much we need it. And only when we emerge on the other side of the storm do we now have the understanding, skill, credibility, and authority to teach others how to find and use their anchor.

I said vision is something we learn to grab hold of when it's tested, but this is also true of all the pillars. The integrity of a building is measured by the degree of stress and weight it can bear, and the same is true of the structure of connection. Love, honor, self-control, responsibility, trust, faith, and vision are wonderful and even essential to aspire to. But they will only ever be as strong as they are when they are put to the test.

What does our love look like when something happens that destroys our sense of safety in a relationship? What does honor look like in the presence of someone's dishonor and disrespect? How do our self-control and responsibility show up when those around us are being out of control and irresponsible? What is our commitment to the truth when trust is violated? Do we choose to rely on the Source when we get depleted, or when those around us are rejecting Him? And do we cling to the vision of who we know we're called to be even when the circumstances, the choices and words of others, or even our own failures want to convince us we're disqualified? These are the questions we must answer—and cannot avoid answering. For we are all in the war of connection, and eventually the fight comes to the door for every one of us. But it's when we answer, and how we answer, that causes these pillars to stand firm.

In the Serpell family, our biggest fight so far in the war of connection started when Delani was in seventh grade. As I described in Chapter 7, the attempted cutting incident that year was our first major alarm bell that a battle between truth and lies had begun in our daughter's heart. As I will narrate in the next chapter, this battle continued through eighth grade and reached a peak of intensity during her freshman year, after which we finally emerged into a much better place. I have decided to share this story with you not because I think our family is unique, but because we're not. The enemy wants all of our kids, plain and simple, and he is great at sneak attacks that blindside us before we can put our pants on in the morning. There were so many moments during that three-year period when Ben and I felt like we had no idea what we were doing. We were getting hit with arrows and then trying to survive the pain while trying to continue to fight for Delani and not add the burden of our own struggle onto hers. That season was messy, excruciating, and full of uncertainty. Our pillar of vision, along with all the other pillars, took hit after hit. Yet in the end, through sheer grace and refusing to let go of the core of our vision—connection—God brought victory, and I know He will do the same for you.

On the other side of those years, what Ben and I carry is deep *hope*. We know the war of connection rages on and that there are battles still to fight for us and each of our children. Yet we know that God is for us. He is on our side and that every time we say yes to Him and to connection, we are standing with the power that is greater than anything the enemy can throw at us. Even in this crazy world of social media and cell phones and technology and distraction and sexual perversion and anti-God culture where we're all trying to raise our kids, there is hope because the power of connection with God, ourselves, and each other will ultimately prove to be stronger, more enduring, more satisfying, and more attractive than any of those things. Connection is what we were made for.

Making connection the central goal, our vision also aligns us with the grace that is greater than our sin, mistakes, and messes. This is the whole message of the gospel: that God sent Jesus to cover and remove every barrier to connection with Him. Jesus has factored our sin into the equation of our sanctification, which means that again, His vision for our lives is not perfection and never making mistakes—it's that His grace is fully sufficient for us and He will perfect His strength through—not in spite of—our weaknesses. As parents, one of our greatest tests of vision is learning to embrace this truth for our children as they encounter challenges, pain, their own weaknesses, poor choices, and consequences. Though we are called to protect them, we cannot sanitize their learning journey of pain and mess. Though we are called to fight for them, we cannot keep them from learning to fight for themselves. We're going to make mistakes as we learn to walk out this tricky balance of staying connected with our kids as they are discovering how to manage their freedom. But as long as we cling to our end of the rope of connection, no matter how painful it gets or how many messes we have to clean up, we will access the grace that brings the breakthrough and victory. So this is my message for you in the next painful, messy, honest, but ultimately victorious chapter as I vulnerably share this season of our lives: *Don't give up hope.*

We build the pillar of vision by:

- Understanding why we need vision
- Recognizing that we really only grab hold of a vision when it costs us something or is painful
- Embracing the truth that our family has a place on the wall to work and fight for the greater vision and mission of the kingdom of God
- Inviting our kids into the process of forming a vision by developing a culture creed and discussing it regularly
- Accepting that the process of living out our vision is messy and full of tests and challenges

9

Our Greatest Fight for Connection (So Far)

ABOUT SIX MONTHS AFTER THE cutting incident, Delani got accepted to a newer charter academy in our city for her eighth-grade year. We were all hopeful she would receive better academic support, find some healthier friends, and overall have a more positive experience than she had had in her first two years of middle school.

Alas, the year ended up getting off to a bumpy start. As I mentioned, our journey of trusting Delani with a cell phone had not been a smooth one. After many talks about trust, freedom, responsibility, and what we expected her to use it for, we decided to allow her to have it again when she started eighth grade. Almost immediately, she made friends with a girl at her new school, exchanged numbers with her, and they started texting. I didn't know anything about the true nature of this relationship for several weeks, until out of the blue I received a call from this girl's mother. After the briefest of introductions, this woman I'd never met began telling me that my daughter was suicidal, that I needed to put her on suicide watch, that she was a horrible influence on the other students at the school, and that we were clearly unfit parents with terrible morals if we were allowing her to behave like this.

Shaking, I stopped this woman mid-sentence, told her the conversation was over, and hung up the phone. I had never experienced this kind of direct verbal attack from a perfect stranger in my life. I took the rest of the afternoon off from work and called a friend to process this blindsiding call before going home to ask Delani what was going on. Thankfully, Ben was home when I got there, and he helped me stay calm as I narrated to Delani what this woman had told me. We asked her to please share with us if she was indeed struggling with suicidal thoughts, what she was looking for, and what she needed from us.

Delani explained that soon after she and this new friend had started texting, she had begun probing into Delani's feelings. Delani had ended up saying some fairly dramatic things about not loving herself and wishing she could change things about herself. She said at one point she had texted something like, "I wish I could either die or be someone else." This girl had then started the rumor that Delani was suicidal, and it had gone around the whole school. The way she had gotten my number was by lying to Delani and saying her mom wanted to invite me to a dinner for moms of students at the school.

We continued to ask questions and eventually Delani agreed that she was not suicidal at all but had just been looking for acceptance and belonging when she sent those emotional texts. She also agreed that she had not made the best choice of friend to get those needs met. We then told her that in our assessment as her parents, the way she had chosen to use her phone suggested she wasn't yet ready to handle the power, freedom, and responsibility of this privilege we had entrusted to her. As her parents, we couldn't control her thoughts, feelings, or choices, but we could control her access to certain permissions, opportunities, and resources, including her phone. We therefore took her phone and explained that we would reassess her having it at a later time when we felt it wasn't too dangerous for her. What a way to start the year!

CROSS COUNTRY

Thankfully, we made it through the rest of eighth grade with no other major incidents, but we continued to experience waves of moods, behavior, connection, and disconnection with Delani. As we had already begun to discern with the cutting incident, our precious daughter was going through the season all kids go through, the season of starting to individuate from us and try to figure out who she is. That was a question we couldn't answer for her, which was frustrating, because we had been able to answer most of her questions pretty well her whole life. But now all we could do was be there whether she was choosing connection or disconnection, present and available, and offer her the truth in hopes that she would choose it among the many other voices and messages that now seemed to be clamoring for her attention.

One thing we knew wouldn't work and would only set us back—though we did stumble and fall into it a few times during these years of battle—was to go into panic mode and resort to fear-driven anger and control. We not only knew this from our own parenting journey but also from our ten-plus years working with kids, youth, and parents as pastors and coaches. Panic leads us to partner with a reaction, not a direction, which means it will inevitably change our goal from connection to self-protection. Self-protection is always fear's goal, though as parents we often mistake it as the desire to protect our kids and easily fall into the trap of letting it steer our thinking and choices. We knew our only hope was to refuse to partner with the fear that was constantly bombarding us and to stay doggedly fixed on the goal of connection, no matter how much frustration, hurt, confusion, or grief we were slogging through.

When Delani started high school, she surprised us by deciding to go out for the cross country team. I thought this was hilarious because up until that point, she had always hated running. Her first meet took place at one of the toughest courses in California, and when she finally crossed the finish line, she was sure she was going to throw up and then die. However, she did neither, and to my surprise, she stuck with the sport. Ben and I were thrilled to see her rising to the challenge. The structure of the team dynamics, weekly practice, and meets were a great way to fill her extra time around school and keep her, as we later realized, from giving that time to less constructive things.

Ben and I did our best to show up for as many races as we could. One of her last races of the season happened to fall right at the end of a weekend trip Ben and I had booked to Australia to surprise his sister for her thirtieth birthday. Yes, I agree that it's insane to go to Australia for a weekend—you spend as much time in the air as you do on the ground. But we wanted to be there for her big day and also back in California for Delani's cross country meet. We had promised her we would do everything in our power to be there at the starting line, so we literally got off the plane, got in the car, and drove straight to the meet. It took us forever to find a parking spot—we had no idea it was one of the biggest meets in the state—but we finally found one and ran to the starting line. Unfortunately, we soon learned from passersby that the race had already started, so we changed directions and posted ourselves about fifty yards from the finish line.

At last, I spotted Delani's distinctive white shorts in the crowd of runners heading toward the finish line. Ben and I both began yelling her name at the top of our lungs and cheering her on. When she saw us, she veered off from the middle of the pack and made a beeline for us on the sidelines. She threw herself into our arms and burst into tears. "I just missed you!" she sobbed. We assured her we would be there to hug her after she finished and urged her back onto the track.

By the time Delani crossed the finish line and reunited with us, I was wiping away tears myself. For two years, we had been navigating the land of tension, of pushing and pulling, where Ben and I kept trying to figure out what our daughter needed and how we could help her as she decided whether she wanted our help or not. But in that moment, it felt like the truth of how much she needed us had broken through. She later told us that when she had passed the first group of bystanders at the start of the race and didn't see us in the crowd, she had collapsed in disappointment. It had taken all her energy to get back up and push through the lies assaulting her: *They didn't make it. They didn't do what they said they'd do. They're not here for me.* So when she saw us on the sidelines, she couldn't help showing how much she wanted the truth to be true. Meanwhile, for Ben and me the message was that our daughter was a girl running a challenging race that we couldn't run for her, but she still needed us. It was a message we especially needed to hear as we entered the most intense part of the battle for connection with Delani. No matter how crazy things got, we had to be there for her on the sidelines.

THE FORBIDDEN HUMAN

Delani finished her final cross country meet and shaved seven and a half minutes off her time from her first race of the season in the process. We were so proud and also felt more connected with her after supporting and cheering her on as she took on this significant challenge in her life. Yet as soon as the season ended, a time vacuum opened in her life, and as it also happened, she now had her phone back after nearly a full year without it.

Toward the end of eighth grade, Delani had started telling us about a certain boy in her class she had begun talking to. At that point it sounded like they were just acquaintances. But as her freshman year progressed, she talked about him more and more, and finally couldn't hide that she was becoming infatuated with him. We responded by saying that while she wasn't allowed to date yet, it was perfectly fine for her to like someone. However, we were completely in the dark about what was actually going on between Delani and this boy until I received an email from the dean of the school notifying me that Delani had been given a detention. This was a first. My best guess was that she hadn't turned in some school work on time. I wrote the dean back and asked, "Can I know what the detention is for?"

Nothing could have prepared me for her reply. "Your daughter was caught making out in the hallway."

Immediately, my thoughts went to a story some good friends of ours had recently told me about their son getting in a strange altercation with this boy Delani had been talking about. At the time, it had sounded like two boys doing some typical chest-puffing, perhaps because our friend's son also liked Delani. Now I put it together that he had probably seen this boy kissing Delani at school and confronted him because he was trying to be protective of her. I tried to imagine my daughter engaged in the kind of flagrant display that would get her caught and put in detention, and I felt pretty provoked myself.

Though the detention was a shock, we had been noticing some worrying behaviors from Delani for several weeks. She had been getting more irritable, snippy with her siblings, and disrespectful toward Ben and me. She had also been spending more and more time in her room with the door closed, and whenever we opened it, she would be on her phone. In fact, she seemed to be obsessively glued to the device at all times. She was also very tired all the time, which we later learned was because she was staying up till 3 a.m. every night texting this boy. So we told her, "You're acting like an addict with this phone, and the Delani we know is disappearing. As soon as you can show us that you can value and reengage with our family, you are welcome to have your phone back."

Whenever we had taken Delani's phone, we had made it clear to her that it wasn't the phone that was the problem—it was the way she was choosing to use this tool to open herself up to other voices and influences and try to get her needs met in ways that were ultimately harmful and destructive. After the cutting and suicide incidents, we had engaged her in many conversations to help her excavate the motives for her behavior and understand why her choices were not going to serve her well. Through that, I believe she had gained some awareness of her deep capacity for empathy, as well as her deep need to be accepted by others. However, her growing attachment to this boy created next-level competition for her heart and attention, and though we didn't know it at the time, the phone had become her link to his acceptance and attraction. Thus, of all the times when we had taken Delani's phone away, this was the most difficult. She was constantly bothered by not having it and constantly angry with us for not letting her have it. Nearly every day she asked, "When can I have my phone back?"

"I would love to give you your phone as soon as you have a plan that helps me feel like a genius for doing so" was my reply.

"This is so stupid!" she would exclaim, rolling her eyes. "What does that even mean?"

"Well, I need to feel safe and feel like I can trust you."

"I don't understand why you can't trust me!"

"Well, I don't love getting notes from the teacher that you are making out with some random boy."

"But why can't I date him?"

"I don't know that I feel like you can handle yourself. I'm pretty scared that if you can't manage yourself at school, then you can't manage yourself alone with him."

"Okay, fine, I won't kiss him anymore!"

Well, she was lying. She was still kissing this boy at school. But what was I going to do? I really did not want to try to surveil or control her, despite her accusations to the contrary. I wanted to invite her to remember, or rediscover, that Ben and I were still there on the sidelines wanting to see her be victorious in this much more difficult race of discovering her own deep identity and emotional needs, as well as her weaknesses. I also believed (incorrectly, it turned out) that even though she was getting away with making some poor choices with this boy, at least she had plenty of adults at school who were keeping an eye on things and making sure things didn't go too far. So I did my best to manage myself in the presence of her constant nagging and disrespect, affirm her, and pursue connection with her in hopes that she would reciprocate. I leaned into her Quality Time love language and took her to get her nails done, to see a movie, to get coffee. She didn't refuse any of these gifts, but she wasn't ready to fully be vulnerable and give me access to her heart.

THE WINTER FORMAL

As we headed into December of that year, things with Delani continued to be strained, and everyone in our home was feeling the effects, not just Ben and me. I wept when I read a letter Adalyn had written to Santa explaining that she didn't want any presents that year—all she wanted was for her sister to be happy again. As much as Ben and I were fighting to protect our family culture and environment, we couldn't fully manage Delani's relationships with her siblings or the damage she was causing as she increasingly became focused on herself and her relationship with this boy.

Meanwhile, I was doing everything I could remember watching my mom do when I lost my mind in high school and dated that boy I met on the internet. She had leaned into pursuing my heart and trying to be present, even in our disagreement. When I heard her retell that story in later years, she said, "I knew that if we took away the one thing that Brittney wanted, she would do everything she could to get it. It was like telling her she couldn't have any more candy after she'd had a taste of it. She was going to find a way to have more of it." All I could think about was, *How am I going to help Delani manage the consumption level of candy in her life and protect her from having an overdose and an outcome that is life-altering?*

So we agreed that she could go to the winter formal as long as Ben was a chaperone and she didn't go with this boy, though we knew he would be there. She was not happy that her dad would be there the whole time watching her. I think deep down she knew that this boy was not pursuing her and treating her with the value that Ben had always shown for her, and she didn't want to be reminded that she was lowering her standards. But of course, she agreed to our terms because she still wanted to go and dance with him.

In an effort to be a cool, supportive mom, I suggested that we get all of Delani's friends together at one of the girls' houses to do their hair and makeup, get their dresses on, and take photos. No sooner were all these girls looking fabulous, then who should show up at the house but a whole group of boys and their moms, including *the* boy and his mom. Now, Delani had told me all about this woman, how amazing and fun she was, and how happy she was about her son's relationship with Delani. Apparently she volunteered at the school, saw Delani frequently there, and would gush to Delani about how she was the best thing that ever happened to her son and that he was so much nicer and more responsible since they'd met. It had been easy to read between the lines and discern that this woman was not an influence I wanted in my daughter's life, and when I saw her, I couldn't help feeling protective anger rise in me. I'm afraid I wasn't a very good Christian that day, because when I met this woman I did not hide in my face that I did not like her and basically saw her as a deceiver trying to lure my daughter away from her home, family, culture, and even God.

As all these freshman boys and girls were taking photos in the driveway, Ben texted me and said he had flowers to give to Delani. So I told her, "Your dad is bringing flowers to you." She didn't want to wait for him, but I insisted she do so. Inside I was thinking, *If you push your dad away right now, you're going to be sad to lose your connection with him, and I'm not going to let you. Your dad is still going to be the anchor who reminds you of who you are—not this boy.* So Ben showed up, gave her the flowers (which she gave to me to take home), and then drove her and several others from the group to the dance.

At home, I waited by my phone for Ben to give me a blow-by-blow of what was happening at the dance. He reported that once they were inside, the boy's mom had whisked him and Delani around to various spots for photos and then started shooting video of them slow dancing together. It was the first time Ben had really seen Delani and this boy interact in person like this, and it did not make him feel good. So Ben decided to ask Delani if she'd dance with him. Even her friends urged her to dance with her dad, but she said she didn't want to. Ben hung back and started talking to another dad there, who encouraged him, "You just need to go over there and dance with your daughter. She needs you to dance with her!" So Ben tried again, and this time Delani let him, though she refused to look at him the whole time.

After this awkward experience, Ben texted me. "I think something sexual has happened between Delani and this boy. I don't know how or what, but the way they look at each other is so intimate. It doesn't feel like a fling."

Well, of course I spent the rest of the evening wondering what could have possibly happened between them. I was 99 percent sure that Delani had only ever seen this boy at school. What could they have done at school?

THE TRUTH COMES OUT

At last, the semester ended and Christmas break arrived. One night we decided to go to the movies, and as we were getting ready, I happened to glance at my phone. To my surprise, there was a notification from "Find My Friends," and when I clicked on it, there was Delani's face lit up like she was in the house with me. Now, at first I didn't understand, because as far as I knew, Delani's phone was completely off and hidden safely in my room in a place she would never find. It had been off since her detention. Slowly it began to dawn on me that no, her phone was very much on, which meant Delani had found it and had it—and had had it for who knows how long.

I calmly walked out of my room and down the hallway to Delani's room, opened the door, and said, "Hey, I know you have your phone. And I need you to go get it."

She just looked at me, probably trying to decide if she was going to lie or not.

"You can get it for me or I can find it myself by looking through your whole room," I said, my voice completely calm and empty of any threatening tone. I was simply informing her of what was about to happen. So she got up, went to the bathroom, pulled her phone out from behind some things in the corner, and handed it to me without a word.

I went back to my bedroom and opened some texts on Delani's phone. There were three or four names I didn't recognize at all. Then I opened a text and saw a photo of Delani lying on her bed in her bra. At that point, I turned the phone off, hid it in a better spot than before, and left for the movies. Somehow, I managed to sit through the movie with Ben, the kids, and Ben's dad, who was visiting from Australia, without losing it. Only after we returned home did I tell Ben that I'd found Delani's phone. We sat together in our room and scrolled through her texts, finding more inappropriate photos of her in the process. It didn't take long before Ben croaked, "Our little girl," and broke down crying, and I soon followed.

Yes, it was our little girl who had made some really poor choices and broken our hearts. At the same time, it wasn't just her. Something had gotten in the door and stolen her innocence, which was infuriating. But we knew we couldn't approach Delani leading either with a broken heart or with anger. This didn't mean completely hiding our emotions in front of her—we had always tried to be honest with her about what we were feeling. However, we had to focus on serving her by finding out what she needed and why she had resorted to these steps to try to meet that need.

So after we had cried and talked about what to do, we brought Delani in our room. I said, "So I'm not sure what to say, or what you need. I've just been crying a lot. But I would love it if you would explain this." I held up her phone.

She looked at us blankly. At last she confessed, "Yeah, I took it. I sent those texts."

"Why?"

"I don't know."

"Okay . . . well. This is really painful. But it's late. So I think we're going to talk tomorrow."

"Fine."

Neither Ben nor I slept much that night, tormented by what we had seen and where it took our imaginations. The next day, we both got up feeling the same pain as the night before. In fact, it would be two weeks before I got up in the morning without feeling an excruciating ache in my chest and immediately starting to cry—after having cried myself to sleep the night before. Have you ever lived through two weeks that felt like an entire year? That's what those two weeks felt like, and it didn't help that it was Christmas. Amid the Delani war zone, our whole family, including my parents and brothers, were home trying to celebrate, and Ben was trying to be present with his dad, who had been going through some painful things in his life. A "holly, jolly Christmas" it was not.

Each day during those two weeks, I entered the fray with my daughter trying to communicate the same message: *Please connect with me. Please let me love you. Please tell me what's going on. Please tell me why you made these choices. Please let me help you figure out what is going on in your heart.* Most of the conversations started with her coming to me and asking if she could have her phone to talk to her friends. Each time, my response was the same. We didn't feel ready to give her the phone, and then I asked her questions. Did she know why she had sent those pictures to this boy? What was she looking for? What was she needing? For days, her answers were either silence or "I don't know," followed by crossed arms, furious tears, and accusations of "You hate me! You're trying to control me! You just want me to be miserable! If you were a better mother, you'd actually trust me!"

By far, these arrows to the heart were the hardest part of the whole battle for me. I had never really understood that one of my greatest fears as a mother was to be rejected and unloved by my own child, until what I feared had come upon me. And it was devastating. I knew she was the child and I was the adult and she was saying things that (I hoped) she would later regret, but it didn't make it hurt any less in the moment. Yet I continued to do my best to hide my tears and pain and respond with love. At the end of each conversation I would say, "I just want you to know that I love you. I am praying for you. Can I touch you? Can I hug you?"

After about a week, Delani finally started to answer the questions differently. I think she had actually been honest in saying she didn't know why she had done what she had done, but now after being confronted repeatedly with the question, she had started to look for the answer. One day she told me, "It just felt good to feel wanted."

"You're right," I said. "It does feel good. I'm just concerned that your definition of being wanted and what he was wanting were not the same thing. Were you wanting to have sex? Because I think that's the message a boy gets when a girl sends him pictures like the ones you sent."

"No, that's not what I want."

"Okay, so what were you looking for?"

Delani ended up admitting that she had secretly had her phone for about two months and had been staying up late every night texting and FaceTiming with this boy. However, it had only been in the week or so before we discovered she had it that she had started sending him pictures. Apparently she had googled, "What is a girl supposed to do for her boyfriend?" The internet had obligingly discipled her on the types of poses a girl ought to send to a guy she liked. She had assumed, with innocent trust, that this was just what you were supposed to do.

Little by little, Delani started to open up more. We discussed whether she was in love with this boy. She said she thought she was, but when I asked her to explain why, she finally admitted that what she loved mostly had to do with the way he made her feel desired and wanted. This led to a conversation about sex. I reaffirmed the message we had consistently taught, which was that sex and sexual desire were good and designed by God, but that design had boundaries. I didn't want her to feel shame for having sexual desires. In the context of a respectful, loving, covenant relationship between a husband and wife, sex is beautiful and a vital part of a whole-life connection. Outside of that context, however, you won't be able to protect and preserve the goodness of sex, I explained. And unfortunately, almost no one on the internet is going to affirm that view of sexuality. The version of sex and relationships promoted by the world is actually deeply unhealthy and disrespectful.

While Delani chewed on this, I came up with a way to find out more about how far she had gone with this boy without having to wade through it myself on her phone and laptop, because my heart just couldn't handle it. I gave both devices to one of my coworkers, who's great with computers, and asked if she would be willing to go through all of Delani's files, emails, and texts and then tell me, without too many details, what I needed to know. How far had she gone with this boy? Had they had sex? Did I need to take her to the doctor? What was the general dynamic of their relationship?

My coworker came back and reported that there had been many pictures and innuendos exchanged between the teenagers, and that this boy had even discussed the idea of them having sex at school, but that she had not found evidence that this had actually happened. Though reassured, I didn't feel fully confident until I asked Delani directly if she had had sex with this boy and if there was any chance she could be pregnant. Her shock at the question was genuine, and I believed her when she said she hadn't and there wasn't. However, after that she began to give me more details of the encounters she had had with this boy at school. After they had discovered certain "blind spots" around the school where they could kiss without being seen, he had become much more handsy with her. He had once touched her breast, upon which she started shaking. However, when he asked what was wrong, she just made faces trying to communicate it was too far. After that, he began trying to touch her inner thigh. However, she didn't know what to say or how to confront his behavior or make it stop. She also said he had asked her repeatedly if she would sneak away with him after the winter formal to make out and perhaps go further physically, despite her explaining that she didn't feel ready for that.

When these confessions came out, I knew we were starting to break through with Delani finally feeling safe enough to be vulnerable and honest with us about what had actually been going on. It was also the point when she started to be honest with herself about the nature of the relationship. She had originally befriended this boy, she realized, because she felt compassion for him when he told her about the brokenness of his home life. He was troubled and always in trouble—apparently he had already been kicked out of several other schools before coming to this one. But once again, her gift for empathy and compassion had opened her up to form an emotional soul tie with someone around their pain, but in this case she had not brought any boundaries to the relationship. Because he was meeting her need to feel wanted, she had excused and complied with his bad behavior and allowed his culture of disrespect and lawlessness to influence her rather than the other way around. The more she saw this, the more she began to admit that their relationship was not healthy and needed to end. Instead of clinging to it, she began to let it go and mourn its loss.

PICK YOUR BATTLES

Once the full truth came out, however, I had a new problem. How was it possible that this boy had been getting away with this behavior at school? Delani said that one incident of him fondling her took place with a teacher present in the room. Were the adults either unaware or turning a blind eye to what was happening? The more I thought about it, the worse I felt about sending Delani back to school without addressing this problem with the dean. So I asked Delani to write out a list of the blind spots around the school and the times and dates when the unwanted, inappropriate touching had taken place, then emailed the dean to ask if she would be willing to meet with us before school resumed.

I'm sure the dean was reluctant to leave the Christmas holidays to deal with a difficult school situation, but she agreed to meet with us. We gave her the letter Delani had put together documenting the touching incidents and explained our concerns. We knew that the kissing and some of the touch had been consensual on Delani's part, and we weren't asking for this boy to be exiled or sent to prison. However, there had been unwanted touch that qualified as sexual assault taking place, and we wanted the school to take steps to monitor these blind spots around the school and make sure my daughter and anyone else was being protected from these things continuing to happen.

A few hours after we left, the dean called me asking for further details about the incidents Delani had described in her letter. The next day, she called the boy and his mother into the office and asked him if the incidents had taken place. At the meeting, he said yes. However, when the dean called the next day to follow up, he denied that they had happened. When the dean told us this, my first thought was that the boy's family had called a lawyer and been coached against confessing to anything. But what was most disconcerting was that the dean then began to discuss the definition of sexual assault with me and suggest that the criteria for assault had not been met if Delani's description of events was true. She had decided we were making a bigger deal of the problem than it was, and the implication was clear—the school would not be tightening security or training teachers to enforce appropriate behavior. In other words, nothing was going to change.

After hitting this wall, we made the decision to keep Delani home from school until I felt safe to send her back there. Delani was initially furious about this and scared she would fall behind in school. However, when I assured her that I would ask the school to send her schoolwork, she calmed down and accepted the decision. By this point, though she missed her other friends, she did have trepidation about being around "the forbidden human," as she would eventually call him, and agreed she was safer at home if no one at the school was going to help look out for her.

To make a long story a little shorter, after a couple weeks of me fruitlessly emailing board members and trying to escalate our complaints to the school's headmistress, a family friend put us in touch with a lawyer who specialized in representing parents when they had a civil or criminal complaint against a school. After hearing our story, he assured Ben and me that we had grounds for a devastating lawsuit against the school if we wanted to pursue it. At that point, we had to clarify what our goal was. We weren't seeking retaliation or retribution. We didn't want to punish this boy or take down the school, even though my mama bear heart of justice was roaring that these entities had failed to protect my daughter. Our real goal was not fighting the world for Delani but helping Delani to figure out who she was so she could eventually go out into the world and fight it herself. So in the end, all we asked the lawyer to do was to write an official letter to the school warning them that if our concerns for Delani's safety were not addressed, legal action could be taken. We were immediately granted a meeting with the head of the school, who told us that while they were not going to take measures to tighten security at the school, they would allow Delani to remain enrolled as an at-home student with full access to her lessons and IEP support until she felt ready to return to school. When she did return, she would be able to meet with the school counselor whenever she needed to discuss any incidents or concerns. We agreed to this plan and set a goal for Delani to return to school by mid-February.

The beauty of this plan is that it didn't come with a list of to-dos or hoops for Delani to jump through. As her parents, we were looking for the fruit of repentance. A month into this whole journey, Delani had apologized to us many times for various things she had done. While there were still days where she was irritable and disrespectful, the hurtful "I hate yous" and accusing comments had totally stopped. I personally witnessed her issuing sincere apologies to both Adalyn and Lincoln for how she had hurt them with mean words and rejection. These were all promising developments. But had she figured out what she needed to do to be able to go back into the school environment and face all the dangers and temptations she was finally beginning to see for what they were?

Unsure of exactly how to discern this myself, I asked my dad what signs to look for in Delani's behavior that told us she was heading in a good direction. He said, "Delani has become consumed with herself. So we're looking for the selfishness to die." My initial thought was, *Waiting for selfishness to die in a teenager? We might be here till she's twenty-five.* But then, one day, we saw it start to happen. All three kids went out to do their daily chores on our farm, which has chickens, goats, and other animals. Lincoln and Adalyn finished theirs quickly and returned to the house, but Delani stayed out for almost an hour. When she got back, I asked her what had taken her so long. She explained that Rosie, one of our goats, had gotten stuck in the tack room, eaten through almost an entire bag of food, and pooped and peed everywhere. "So I had to clean it all up and then hose and dry it out," she concluded.

After Delani had gone upstairs to change, I gave meaningful looks to Ben and my parents, who were in the kitchen with me. They all knew that chores, and especially anything involving cleaning up poop, were among Delani's least favorite things to do. Yet instead of running into the house and complaining to me that the goat had made a mess and I needed to deal with it, she had simply done it herself. My dad spoke up and said, "That's what we're looking for."

TRANSFORMATION

A few days before the date we had set with the school for Delani's return, we were granted a gift. The head of the school informed us that the boy had been expelled from the school. Delani and I immediately burst into tears, relieved that this one obstacle in the midst of all the other ones was no longer there.

Delani did half days her first week back at school to ease into it. The next Monday, I picked her up after her first full day back and was surprised when she started crying. My first thought was that someone had bullied, mocked, or threatened her.

"What's going on, honey?" I asked, silently adding, *Who do I need to kill?*

"I just missed you all day," was her tearful reply.

Wow. In two months—okay, they had been the longest two months of my life—we had gone from my daughter saying, "I hate you!" to "I missed you all day!"

That was mid-February of 2020. Less than two months after that, the school shut down for the COVID-19 pandemic, and all our kids came home. Delani never ended up returning to that school, as we found a private online academy we loved and enrolled her there. But even as the world slipped into chaos and panic day by day, in the Serpell house we were witnessing our firstborn daughter transforming into someone who was now convinced that her parents and her siblings loved her, were for her, and after God, were the strength she could pull on to help her continue to navigate her journey to adulthood. Instead of seeing the rope linking her boat with ours as a restriction, she now saw it as a resource, which she demonstrated by continuing to pursue and protect connection with us. She became fully engaged once again in her relationships with each of us, and we saw more and more unselfish, kind, and thoughtful behavior coming out of her. We also were thrilled to see her renew her pursuit of the Lord, willingly choosing to read the Word, pray, and worship with passion at church.

About a year after we had taken Delani's phone away, we decided to give her another one, this time with stripped-down features and limited access to the internet. We took her out to dinner and gave her the phone, along with a purity ring featuring two pink stones on either side of a diamond, and invited her to consider making a new commitment to honor God's design for sexual purity before marriage. "The diamond represents you, because you are rare and beautiful," I said. "The pink stones are Daddy and me on one side of you, and the Father on the other side." When we got home from dinner, a group of youth leaders and friends who had walked alongside us and Delani through this whole journey were waiting there to meet us. We all prayed and prophesied over Delani and took communion together. It was a sacred and precious time.

Thankfully, Delani has chosen to honor our trust in giving her a phone again. She has faced more opportunities to get caught up in distracting herself with it, as well as opportunities to get sucked into friend drama, and even an opportunity to date another boy. But on the other side of the great battle for connection that fateful Christmas, the difference is that she has never again let go of her end of the rope with us. As a result, she has been learning to set personal and emotional boundaries that help protect her and her most important relationships. She even broke things off with that second boy when it became clear that he could not align with and respect certain values our family holds. I should also mention that she read and contributed to writing this chapter with me, giving me permission to tell this very personal story because she understands the impact this story can have for parents. She wants to encourage both parents and teenagers not to stop pursuing connection, even when it's so hard. I absolutely love my daughter's tender and compassionate heart for people! I hope I can be more like her one day.

Delani recently wrote a paper for school in which she explained that Ben and I are her best friends, and her favorite thing is when Ady and Lincoln sleep over at friends' houses so she can stay up and hang out with us, go out to dinner, or watch a show together. When I read it, all I could feel was deep gratitude for the grace of God that had brought us to that point. In the heat of the battle, I couldn't really see or feel it, but that grace was there, fighting for us, giving us the ability we couldn't have had on our own to resist collapsing under the pain, fear, and anger, and to believe in hope that no matter how trapped in lies our daughter had become, the Holy Spirit could and would set her free and bring her back to the truth.

Yes, choosing to keep our love on and stay engaged in the fight was costly. I gave up several months of work to put Delani into what was essentially a 24/7 detox and rehab for her heart and emotions, and only those closest to me understood or approved of what I was doing. I understand why so many parents in these kinds of situations become exhausted, discouraged, and confused when things aren't changing and when everyone around them, from their child to their friends, the world, and even many in the church, are telling them that the loving thing is not to fight but to let go. But love never lets go. As 1 Corinthians 13:7 says, "Love never takes failure as defeat, for it never gives up" (TPT).

Fully engaged love is the only thing that can shatter the enemy's lies over our children. Just as the enemy did with us, he is trying to sow seeds of rejection, fear, abandonment, and lack of identity in our kids so they walk the earth as spiritual orphans, vulnerable to seeking their heart's desires and needs in destructive ways and places. But when we stay fully engaged with our love, pursuing connection always over perfection or control, we show our children the Father. We become an undeniable manifestation of the truth that they are unconditionally and sacrificially loved, wanted, believed in, protected, provided for, and known. There is no greater honor or worthier cause than this, for this is what empowers them with the courage to grow up and have their own children and raise them in this love so the legacy of connection continues. So, no matter how intense the fight feels or how overwhelming your failures seem as a parent, don't give up. "Don't be afraid of the enemy! Remember the Lord, who is great and glorious, and fight for your brothers, your sons, your daughters, your wives, and your homes!" (Nehemiah 4:14 NLT). He's got you, and you've got this.

10

Go Home and Love Your Family

I DON'T KNOW ABOUT YOU, but in our family we love epic movies about courage and heroism—especially ones like *Braveheart* or *The Lord of the Rings* with iconic scenes where the king or general rallies his troops to battle with a great speech and a war cry. As I reached the final pages of this book, I knew I had just a bit more to say. I wanted and needed to send you off with a full war cry of my own.

Parents, we are in a war. Perhaps this reality has not yet fully come home to you. If so, I don't want you to be vulnerable and caught off guard. The enemy has a plan for your family, and he knows he can win if you do not engage in the fight.

Or perhaps you have already been blindsided by his attacks and you're reeling and weary from the fight. Perhaps you have already started to believe that you have no hope of victory. If so, I want you to know that *there is always hope*. You just have to reach for it.

In the most intense season of our fight for connection with Delani, I woke up many mornings weeping, wondering if I even had the strength to get out of bed. I knew I didn't have the strength I needed in myself, but I knew I could reach for the Source of strength and hope. And so, through my tears and pain, I turned to the Word of God and the Holy Spirit.[5] Every time, I found Him there, waiting and ready to breathe fresh life into my spirit. He will do the same for you—you only need to call Him.

THE FOUNDATION OF HOPE

One verse that I learned to cling to in the height of the battle was Psalm 31:24: "Be strong and take heart, all you who hope in the Lord" (NIV). *That's me,* I reminded myself. *I put my hope in Him.* But what does it mean to put our hope in the Lord as parents? Well, that is something that only really becomes clear in the fight.

The first thing that becomes clear is that our hope cannot depend on our performance or doing everything perfectly as parents. We will make mistakes, and when we do and things blow up in our faces, it can fill us with self-doubt. I don't know how many times during that three-year period I found myself saying, "Wow, that conversation did not go the way I had hoped. Am I doing this right? Should we have tried again in a different way?" Now, if we swim in these doubts and allow them to convince us to disqualify ourselves and disengage from the fight, then the enemy wins. He wins when we get confused and forget who we are, what we're called to do, Who we're partnered with, and the resources we have. That's what he wants.

But from God's perspective, it's essential that any hope we're putting in ourselves, our performance, or anything but Him is shaken. He is inviting us through the disappointment, disillusionment, and self-doubt to discover the second thing that becomes clear in the battle, which is that the only true foundation upon which our hope can rest is Him and Him alone.

---

[5] Verses that helped me in this season: Lamentations 3:22-24, Isaiah 54:10, Isaiah 54:13-14, Isaiah 59:21, Jeremiah 1:5, Habakkuk 2:2, Proverbs 1-2-4, Psalm 119:27-29, Psalm 78:1-8, Psalm 27:6-7, Psalm 31:24, Daniel 3

The more we put our hope in the Lord, the more we find the firm ground on which to plant our feet—the unshakable truths that God has actually called and appointed us to this fight, that He is our partner in the battle, and that He will bring us victory and success in our assignment to fight for the hearts of our children.

One of my favorite things I have ever heard my mother say is, "You are the perfect parent for your child. No one could ever have loved them more than you." Despite every flaw you have, every mistake you've made, every mess that's come from a situation, the reality is that God chose you to be the mother or father of your child. He knew you were capable, because He equipped you with everything needed to fulfill this job and planned to grow your capacity as you learned to partner with Him. God says of you as He said to the prophet Jeremiah, "Before I formed you in the womb I knew you, before you were born I set you apart" (Jeremiah 1:5 NIV). You were formed and set apart to be the mother or father of your child. God chose you and trusted you with the greatest privilege and honor in the world—to partner with the Father and be the first mirror and experience of who He is to our children. We get to show them that He fights for us, protects us, and never gives up.

FLY, FIGHT, CROW

The classic Stephen Spielberg film *Hook,* starring Robin Williams, is a favorite in our house for many reasons, but for me, it's one of the best imaginative depictions of the war of connection we're in as parents—and how we achieve victory. In particular, it shows how God is committed to helping us recover our identity, our assignment, our weapons of warfare, and our passion for the fight when they have been lost.

Williams plays Peter Banning, an unengaged father who puts work, others' priorities, and himself before his family. However, we soon discover that he is, in fact, Peter Pan, who has grown up and forgotten his true identity. The action takes off when Peter's two children, Maggie and Jack, are abducted by none other than the infamous Captain Hook—just think of him as the devil—who leaves a note for Peter saying he is holding them hostage until Peter returns to Neverland to fight him.

The problem is that Peter has not only forgotten he's Peter Pan; he's forgotten everything. He doesn't even believe there is a Neverland or Captain Hook anymore. What ultimately starts to reawaken him to the truth is the arrival of Tinker Bell, a fiery, spicy, electrifying little fairy who magnificently represents the Holy Spirit in this movie. Tinker Bell drags Peter to Neverland and brings him right to the ship where Captain Hook has Maggie and Jack trapped in a rope net dangling from a mast. Hook can't believe that this grownup, pathetic man is actually Peter Pan, so he gives him a test—if he can climb the mast and reach out to touch the fingers of his kids, Hook will release them. Peter climbs, but once he gets out on the boom, his fear of heights kicks in and he can't bring himself to stretch his arm out to their reaching hands. In that instant, Jack and Maggie see that their father cannot overcome his own fears to fight for them, and their eyes fill with sadness and hopelessness. It's the moment where we see what a shell and counterfeit of himself Peter has become. The real Peter Pan could fly—this Peter is afraid of heights!

Yet in this moment of failure and defeat, Tinker Bell steps in. She tells Hook, "Give me three days, and I will prove that he is the real Peter Pan and get him into fighting shape." Three days! It's Jesus' resurrection all over again. So Hook throws Peter overboard, leaving it up to Tink to work out how to help him.

Tinker Bell takes Peter back to the Lost Boys, who initially scoff at the idea that he's the real Peter Pan, but then decide to give him a chance. They then begin to rally around him and remind him of what it means to be "the Pan." Specifically, the Pan can fly, he can fight, and he can *crow* (a great metaphor for using the power of our voices). Like prophetic intercessors, the Lost Boys begin to not only call out Peter's identity but also get him into intensive battle training to recover these three unique abilities tied to that identity.

The scenes with the Lost Boys beautifully depict the role of community in giving us the strength and courage we need for the fight. Part of why Peter has forgotten his identity is that he has forgotten the community he belonged to—he without the Lost Boys has become truly lost! Again, in God's design for His family and our families, our individual identity and role are connected to the whole. When we become cut off and separated from that, we become lost and disempowered. I know from personal experience that when you go through hard things without community, the only thing that grows louder is your sense of failure. Like-minded people help us fight our battles. When we can't hear the Holy Spirit or find hope in His Word, we need others around us to be our Aaron and hold our arms up when we are growing weary. So stay connected to the body of Christ, because you never know when you need your people to remind you of who you are.

Along with community, the Holy Spirit is the other one who reminds us of who we are. In the movie, Peter has his big identity breakthrough through an encounter with Tink (the Holy Spirit) that causes him to remember everything—all the way back to when he was an infant Tink rescued and brought to Neverland in the first place. He also remembers why he left Neverland and grew up, which was that he wanted to be a father. Maggie and Jack are his "happy thought"! As soon as he finds his happy thought, he can fly!

With his identity, his supernatural abilities, and his reason to fight restored, Peter returns to confront Hook. There he discovers that Hook has spent the last three days grooming his children, particularly Jack, poisoning them against their father, and getting them to identify Hook as their father instead. When you see Jack, he is even dressed like Hook in the same iconic wig and coat. When Peter first returns, his own son doesn't recognize him and asks Hook, "Who is that?" That's the power of the deceiver. He wants our children to not even recognize our heart for them. They begin to see us, as well as the Father, as their enemy. I do think it was significant that Jack, more than Maggie, succumbed to the enemy's lies and lost his identity. Because boys grow up to be fathers, and as Ben says, "Fathers set the level of love in the home." But that is for another book.

Now convinced that Peter is indeed "the Pan," Hook and his army begin to fight Peter and the Lost Boys. As Peter is dueling Hook, he looks at his son and reminds him who "Jack" is. It's not long before Jack looks at himself, realizes this is not who he is, and begins to take off the jacket and wig he's been wearing. Peter's restored identity enables him to restore his son's identity! The battle ends with Hook defeated and Peter winning his children back. Best of all, when he returns from Neverland to the "real" world, he is a changed man and father. He throws his work cell phone out the window and embraces his family, their love and connection restored and the priority of connection firmly established in his heart.

LOVE YOUR FAMILY

I love how this film depicts the reality of growing up in a fallen world. We have all been blinded by the "real." We have forgotten or failed to perceive the spiritual battle in the unseen and our role in that battle. But God has not forgotten it, and He is committed to helping us remember who He is, who we are, and what our assignment is. Our assignment is just what it always was—to partner with Him in making a connected, loving family and subduing the earth.

The contrast between the Peter who failed to reach out and touch his children and the Peter who flew to fight and rescue them cannot be greater. It's a clear picture of the transformation that's available to us once we truly remember who we are and recover our powers and passion for the fight.

One of the biggest places we can see this transformation unfolding is in our prayers. When we feel lost in the battle, the best we can do is to cry, "Help!" Many times we don't even do that, because we've forgotten the Holy Spirit is our partner in the fight. But once we know who we are and that we have all of heaven behind us, we become bold. Even when we see our children becoming disconnected, pulling away, and held captive by lies, we go to the Lord and say, "Lord, You gave me these children. You've equipped me to lead them, steward them, guide them, and discipline them. The enemy has no authority over them. Break every lie that is attacking them now in Jesus' name. Show me how to partner with You in displaying the truth of Your heart and my heart for them." We step into the authority that is ours through who God is, who He says we are, and what He has commissioned us to do, and we wield that authority in the spiritual and natural realm to win the fight.

God is not going anywhere and He's got our kids forever. One of my favorite verses is, "'As for me, this is my covenant with them,' says the Lord. 'My Spirit, who is on you, will not depart from you, and my words that I have put in your mouth will always be on your lips, on the lips of your children and on the lips of their descendants—from this time on and forever,' says the Lord" (Isaiah 59:21). One of the dreams that inspires me most is to imagine an entire church, community, or even a nation of families who are walking fully in this generational covenant with the Spirit and Word of God, who know their individual identity in the body of Christ, who are fighting in their authority and mature love to drive away fear and deception, and who are committed to the goal of building and protecting connection at all costs. When we know who we are and what we walk in, take our stand on the wall, and tell the enemy, "You shall not pass," I believe we will shake the gates of hell.

And so, I leave you with the words of Mother Teresa: "What can you do to promote world peace? Go home and love your family."